ARMADA STRATEGIES for SPANISH 21

Sink the Casinos' Hottest New Game

FRANK SCOBLETE

Bonus Books, Inc.
Chicago, Illinois

This book is dedicated to the memory of

Lenny Frome

"In those days, there were giants in the earth...."
Genesis, 6:4

© **1998 by Bonus Books, Inc.**
All rights reserved

02   01   00   99   98   5   4   3   2   1

Library of Congress Cataloging Card Number 98-72687

ISBN 1-56625-106-0

Bonus Books, Inc.
160 East Illinois Street
Chicago, Illinois 60611

Printed in the United States of America

Acknowledgments

First a big thank you to blackjack expert Fred Renzey, the author of *Blackjack Bluebook*, who helped me analyze the game of Spanish 21 and whose advice and recommendations upon reading the manuscript were instrumental in making this book complete and comprehensive. Also thank you to my wife and partner in adventure, the beautiful A.P. (Alene Paone) without whom my success would be as so much dust in the wind. Thank you once again to Aaron Cohodes, my publisher at Bonus Books, for taking a shot with an unknown author in 1991. Finally to my editors at Bonus, Andrea Lacko and Elena Darden, a thank you for always responding promptly to my queries and concerns.

"Experience keeps a dear school, but fools will learn in no other."

...Benjamin Franklin

Table of Contents

1

The Spanish Armada and Blackjack

In the year 1588, King Philip II of Spain decided that he would prove to the annoying British that God was in fact a Catholic and not one of these newfangled Protestants. It seems that those upstart Protestants in England, under the benign auspices of the aggressive Queen Elizabeth I, were also honing in on Spanish loot that was being taken from the colonies in America. Those pesky British even had the audacity to attack Spanish ships at sea and steal their booty. And, as everyone knows, you never steal another man's booty.

So Philip decided to show that God was on Spain's side by building some of the biggest, best, and most impressive ships ever seen and sailing these to England to send those Brits a message that they would not soon forget. But Philip himself had forgotten a very important thing. Man does not set up the criteria for God's displays of power or preference. The Bible that all three Western religions believe in says quite clearly on a number of occasions: "Man shall not put God to the test!" It is presumptuous. It smacks of hubris. Besides, God might get irritated and decide to have a little fun with you. So, while Philip might have been interested in showing that God was a Catholic, God Himself didn't seem particularly thrilled with the idea and even sent Philip a clear message to let him know that perhaps he should forget this whole Armada thing. Before the first Armada could even get out of the Spanish port of Cadiz, Sir Francis Drake, Britain's greatest seaman, had sailed in and sunk a few Spanish ships for good measure. That should have made anyone with half a brain realize that maybe this Armada thing wasn't such a good idea. God wasn't even being subtle in this particular case.

Unfortunately, if King Philip had been a car (to mix time periods), it would even be obvious to an unschooled mechanic that all his cylinders weren't firing properly. Instead of taking God's hint, Philip just redoubled his efforts to build the biggest, best, and most awesome assemblage of ships ever seen. Unfortunately, while big and impressive to the eye, many of the ships Philip built were actually slow-moving monstrosities that found themselves unable to cope with the speedier, streamlined British fighters. Many of Philip's top seamen tried to explain to him that he was indeed a complete idiot for trying to build such an Armada, although they didn't quite call him an idiot to his face. While couching their criticism in *"your majesty, your highness,* perhaps, *your great one,* you should, *oh lord and master,* consider that, *glorious one,* the English, *oh mighty King,* might, *oh heavenly power,* kicketh, *oh wondrous one,* our collective, *my liege,* buttocks including, *great king,* our codpieces, *your lordship"*—it amounted to the same thing: "King, you are one big jerk if you keep persisting with this Armada thing!"

But Philip was determined to have his Armada and sail it too. Instead of putting a great and experienced seaman in command (the Spanish had several of these), he appointed the one man who absolutely didn't want the job, a totally inexperienced seaman, the Duke of Medina Sidonia, whose only great success in naval battles took place in his bathtub with toy ships. According to neighbors, when Sir Sidonia attempted the same feat with his toy ships at the local lake, many of them sank. When Sidonia was appointed to head the great Armada, these same neighbors heard him say (in Spanish): "Oh, crap!"

He was the perfect choice for Philip.

The Spanish Armada left Lisbon, Portugal (which was occupied by Spain) on May 30, 1588 with 130 ships and returned to Spain several months later with just 67 ships, most of them badly crippled. Sidonia was heard to say: "I had more luck at the lake."

British Protestants rejoiced and Philip wondered why God had played him for the fool.

Which brings me to blackjack.

For years now, the casinos have tried to float new games on the casino playing ocean. Most of these games have ended up like the Spanish Armada, in the drink, because they were cumbersome vessels with high house edges. Swift players treated these new games the way the swift British ships treated the lumbering Armada, they sank them. Pokette, Russian Roulette, Casino War, Two Up, Hickok's Six Card have all sailed out of the casino docks with high hopes only to return crippled or not at all.

Still, like the persistent King Philip, the casino executives continue to introduce new games in the hope that some of them will float. Some games have actually succeeded: Let It Ride, Caribbean Stud, and Three Card Poker [see my book, *Bold Card Play: Best Strategies for Caribbean Stud, Let It Ride, and Three Card Poker*]. But for every Let It Ride success, there are hundreds of "Let It Die" failures that are introduced. But new games are to the casinos what that Armada was to King Philip—an obsession.

This is particularly true in blackjack, where the fact that some card-counting players can get an edge over the casinos has rankled these same executives to no end. The fact that these edges are rather small and have not significantly hurt the take at the blackjack tables is irrelevant. You can even make a strong case that ever since it became general knowledge that a few players can beat the game, blackjack profits have actually soared to unparalleled heights. Still, casino executives do not want casino players to have any of their booty. In this, they are also like King Philip. Although blackjack makes more money for the casinos than any other table game (industry statistics show that 10 to 15 percent, and sometimes more, of all the money played at blackjack eventually winds up in the casino treasury) it seems this is not enough to content the King Philips of the industry. They are determined to prove that the god of casino table games is not *blackjack* but...whatever *they* can come up with as a substitute game. Thus, blackjack variations, most of them heavily favoring the house over ill-informed players, have been floated more often than any other vessel (over-under 13, royal match, multiple action, double exposure, and jackpot blackjack, just to name a few). Most have either died early deaths or gained a small toehold, much like a barnacle on the bottom of a boat, but not one has come along to seriously challenge basic blackjack's popularity.

Until now that is.

Finally, after years of trying and years of failing to come up with a strong alternative to traditional blackjack, the casinos seem to have succeeded with their newest entry called, appropriately enough, Spanish 21 or Spanish Blackjack. In my many visits to Las Vegas, I have seen more and more players at these tables. Many have told me with a confident smile: "This is a much better game than blackjack. It's more fun and better for the players. You have so many choices and options that you don't have at regular blackjack. Regular blackjack is much duller by comparison." Spanish 21 is therefore one ship that is staying afloat because it is fast, sleek, evidently offers many players what they want, and has a reasonable house edge, if the players know what they are doing, and a rather substantial house edge if the players don't. Unfortunately, most of the players don't know what they're doing.

On the face of it then, Spanish 21, conceived and created by Richard Lowfink, with Julian Braun doing the initial mathematical combinatorial analysis (you might recognize Braun's name as he is the same Julian Braun who is the father of basic blackjack strategy) is one Armada that will successfully navigate the rough waves of the casino seas without going under or being crippled. In fact, Mr. Lowfink has created a game that is fun, fast-paced, and almost impregnable to players beating it in the long run with traditional advantage-play methods such as card counting—which is just what the casinos ordered. To the casino potentates *God is a blackjack game that can't be beaten by anyone under any circumstances!*

Yet, with the proper basic strategies for the play of the hands (strategies quite different from regular blackjack), Spanish 21 can be considered a very good game as casino games go for it has a reasonable 0.82 percent house edge. What does that edge mean? For every $100 that you wager at Spanish 21, you will lose a mere 82 cents in the long run! Compared to American roulette ($5.26 lost per $100 wagered), Let It Ride ($2.80 lost per $100 wagered), and Pai Gow

Poker ($2.50 lost per $100 wagered) and the Pass Line at craps ($1.41 per $100 wagered), 82 cents lost per $100 wagered is a very low edge indeed. Yet, Spanish 21 is racking up the money from most casino players because they are employing the wrong tactics against it. They are playing a mutant form of blackjack with the old strategies that were created for the traditional one. These traditional basic blackjack strategies are to Spanish 21 what the Armada was to the Spanish—a substantial loss just waiting to happen. Play traditional blackjack strategies at Spanish 21, or worse, play your own version of what you think the best Spanish 21 strategy should be, and you are asking for trouble, big trouble. In fact, you're asking to be swallowed by the abyss.

The Nature of Spanish 21 vs. Traditional Blackjack

Spanish 21 and traditional blackjack do have many things in common. The basic thrust and conditions of the games are the same; the basic goals are similar, as are the card values and procedures. These I will discuss in chapter 2. However, Spanish 21 and traditional blackjack share something else that is also quite important—both games are considered "dependent" trial games, which makes them games where the players' decisions have a major impact on the players' economic expectations. Yet, one, traditional blackjack, can be beaten in the long run by skillful, traditional, advantage play, while the other, Spanish 21, for all practical purposes cannot. (Don't despair, dear reader, because the Armada Strategies, which include the Armada Play of the hands and the Armada Ruse for gaining comps can often turn the game into a favorable *economic* one for the players as you shall see in chapter 7.)

One of the best descriptions I have ever read as to what makes traditional blackjack such a good game comes from Fred Renzey's excellent volume *Blackjack Bluebook* (Chicago Spectrum Press):

[Blackjack] is different [because] it is one of the few casino games in which the player uses his judgment to make decisions *after* his bet has been placed. These decisions will either increase or decrease his chance of winning the bet. For example, if you always stand when you have a 2-4-Ace against a dealer's 4 up, you'll only win 46 percent of those hands, but if you hit you'll win 53 percent of them. Hence, for you blackjack may be the best game in the house, or the worst one depending upon how well or how poorly you make your decisions.

....the game of blackjack is more than a century old. When its rules were first structured, putting the house at an advantage was much more complicated than just paying 35 to 1 on a 37 to 1 shot [as is the case in American roulette]. The game's inventors had no computers to determine what the exact percentages would be in many of the more extreme nuances that can arise in a blackjack hand. Instead, they had to work from a more fundamental set of mathematical probabilities realizing that the player, too, would be limited by his own reasoning powers. That being the case, the available design tools of their day were sufficient to provide the house with a comfortable edge over any human of that era. And so it went for several decades. Then came the age of computers.

Today's computer-derived playing strategies for blackjack extend well beyond the players' own perceptive logic. In a casino gambling arena, where the house advantages on the table games average about 3 percent, a well-informed blackjack player gives up just a 0.5 percent edge to the house in a typical multi-deck game by doing nothing more than memorizing a basic strategy chart. A 0.5 percent disadvantage means playing 200 hands and finishing one bet behind if the odds run true to form. I don't think it was ever intended to be that close of a contest.

The second big difference about blackjack is that, unlike craps and roulette, it is a game of 'dependent' events. That means that once you've been dealt a 4 and a 3, then hit it with a deuce, deuce, 5 and a 6 for example, those cards go into the discard rack and *cannot* be dealt again for the remainder of the shoe. As the cards grow more and more depleted, sometimes certain hands become easier to make and certain other hands grow more scarce. In fact, there are times when your chances of being dealt a blackjack are 1 in 17, and other times when they are 1 in 25. It's like knowing that the number 10 in craps now has a 1 in 9 chance of coming up rather than the normal 1 in 12.

Spanish 21 shares with its traditional parent the fact that deck composition changes the expected outcomes. However, unlike traditional blackjack, Spanish 21 was developed in a time *with* computers, and *with* advanced mathematical analysis, and *with* the goal in mind that the game would be absolutely impregnable to traditional player assaults such as card counting. To make it an unbeatable game—and again for all *practical* purposes it *is* an unbeatable game if we approach it in a traditional way—the casinos brought in heavyweight mathematicians and computer experts to run simulations and construct mathematical models of a blackjack game that would look and feel like a better version than its parent, but would have an entirely different and a not-so winning personality. The creators of Spanish 21 designed a game that would be appealing, exciting, *seemingly advantageous* to the players, but would, in effect, be unsinkable by card counters and other traditional "advantage" players looking to get the edge. Where the original blackjack was a card game that evolved over time; Spanish 21 is a laboratory clone that has been genetically altered to bring out certain traits and suppress other traits.

The main trait was that no gaming writer such as myself would be able to come up with a way to beat it. This they largely succeeded in doing if we approach Spanish 21 in a straight line traditionalist way. Now, while there are times when it might be *theoretically* possible to get a tiny edge at Spanish 21 by traditional methods and exploit that edge in the traditional ways, it is *practically* impossible to do so. (And thus the need for my nontraditional Armada Strategies.)

Here's how Spanish 21 was structured to be a mutant that couldn't be killed, or an Armada that couldn't be sunk:

The first step was to make the game a shoe game. For the typical traditional basic strategy player, a six-deck shoe game in blackjack has about a 0.5 percent edge for the casino. The second step the designers took was to strip the decks of all the 10-spot cards, leaving just the jack, queen, and king as 10-*valued* cards. Without any subsequent rule changes, the effect of stripping the decks of 25 percent of the 10-valued cards would be devastating for the players. A blackjack basic strategy player faces a whooping 2.5 percent disadvantage (in some cases even more) when playing against such a six-deck shoe. However, even the dumbest blackjack player would pass up a black-jack game where 25 percent of all the 10-valued cards were removed and nothing was given in return.

So the inventors of the game came up with ingenious and enjoy-able rewards for certain premium hands such as five, six and seven-card 21s, player 21s beating dealer 21s and the like. Such hands, which are among the most frustrating in regular blackjack, now become a source of great joy for the Spanish 21 players. The inventors gave just enough back in the form of "perks" to make the game an attractive lure for players who were either tired of traditional black-jack, or for players who were looking to leave the machine world and journey to the tableland.

Even with the rewards that were added to the game, a tradi-tional blackjack player would still be courting a swift sinking by attempting to play Spanish 21 using the traditional multiple-deck basic strategy that has appeared in all the worthwhile blackjack books for the past thirty years. Many of the more economically rewarding moves in traditional multiple-deck blackjack strategy, such as doubling on an 11 against a dealer's 10, 9, or 8, have devas-tating consequences when employed against Spanish 21.

So why would anyone prefer Spanish 21 to traditional black-jack? Because its personality is radically different than its more dour parent. Players love to make choices and players love to win more money than they originally laid out—two factors that have con-tributed to the explosion of video-poker games over the past decade. Spanish 21 gives the players both—there are plenty of choices to make and there are plenty of hands where you get more bangs for your bucks than in traditional blackjack. In addition, if you learn the proper basic strategy for Spanish 21—the Armada Play basic strat-egy—you will be playing a tight game with the casino. That 0.82 per-cent edge is damn good when compared to most other casino games, as I've stated.

Yet....

The casinos are not really giving the players much of a crack at playing such a tight game because of two factors: player inertia and player stupidity. The Armada Play basic strategy for Spanish 21 is much more complicated than the basic strategy for traditional black-jack. The casinos are fully aware of this and they are also aware of the fact that most people are not going to bother learning this compli-cated new strategy. Instead, the unwary and unwise players will play the traditional blackjack strategy against Spanish 21 and give the casinos edges in the 2 to over 3 percent range. Other players, perhaps fancying themselves to be more astute than the casinos, will invent hybrid variations of traditional basic strategy to employ against the hybrid Spanish 21—with equally devastating effects on their bankrolls.

Thus, the need for this book.

Unlike many gaming books that I've written, *Armada Strategies for Spanish 21* is geared to two radically different gaming publics. On the one hand, there are Group One Players, who comprise the tradi-tional basic-strategy players in blackjack and who are now flirting with this new game because it offers a level of excitement not found in the traditional blackjack games. These players already know the basics of the game of blackjack—how it's played and how to, more or less, correctly play it—and are just looking for ways to improve their chances against this new and, to them, improved version of the game.

Group Two Players, on the other hand, are composed of those players who have never played traditional blackjack but are flirting with jumping from other table games that they are currently playing (Caribbean Stud, Let It Ride, etc.) because they have assumed (cor-rectly) that Spanish 21 offers them a better bang for their bucks. Included in this group are slot and video-poker players who are look-ing to make the leap—or the leap back—to the table games.

And what about traditional blackjack card counters and advan-tage players, who generally play with edges of between 0.5 and 1.5 percent—where do they fall into this mix? In my opinion, they don't, unless they want to approach the game with a whole different mind-set. While it is theoretically possible to get a small edge (around a 0.5 *at the most*) at Spanish 21 by employing traditional card counting techniques, to do so requires a minimum to maximum bet spread of at least 1 to 30—an almost impossible spread in the real world of casi-nos and one that is impossible for most players to afford to make. For most of the game a $10 minimum bettor who is counting cards at

Spanish 21 will be betting that $10 minimum because the game does not favor him. However, the few occasions when the game favors him (which is maybe 5 percent of the time), he will have to pump those bets to $300 to realize even that tiny edge. Such a betting spread, while not theoretically impossible, is extremely dangerous as a bad streak could wipe out most players' bankrolls in short order. To attempt to play Spanish 21 with an advantage in the traditional way would therefore require a bankroll of enormous proportions. However, to be thorough, I will discuss the possibility of card counting at Spanish 21 in chapter 5.

Of the two groups of players, believe it or not, the novice Group Two Players—those who have *never played* traditional blackjack—will probably have a better time of it than those who are already players of the parent game, because the novice won't have to unlearn traditional basic strategy moves. For the novice, hitting a hand of 12 against a dealer's upcard of 5 or 6 won't seem so bizarre or frightening, but to the traditional player such a move might just give him or her heart palpitations as this is never done in the regular version of blackjack. In fact, make a move such as hitting a 12 against a dealer upcard of 5 or 6 at a traditional blackjack table and you risk an explosion of ire and derision from the other players at the table.

How to Read This Book

This book has two distinct thrusts. It will teach the novice how to play Spanish 21 from scratch and it will inform the experienced blackjack player of the differences between the traditional game and the new one. Although I will, as stated, discuss methods of card counting at Spanish 21, if you are a card counter having success with the traditional game, it would not benefit you to play Spanish 21, unless you were doing so for cover and for relatively small stakes. You might also want to play Spanish 21 for fun—again for much lower stakes than you would play at when you were attacking traditional blackjack.

For all players, I will delineate a new basic strategy for the play of every player hand against every dealer upcard for Spanish 21, which I have dubbed *The Armada Play* [chapter 3]. The Armada Play, coupled with certain money management and time management principles that I discuss, will go a long way to giving you an excellent shot at taking home some money in what seems to be an ever more popular game. In fact, if you can accurately employ the strategy called the *Armada Ruse* [chapter 7] into your game plan, you might even be able to get a *monetary* edge over the casino!

Traditional Group One players, you are going to be asked to do things that will make your hair stand on end, such as the aforementioned hitting on 12 against a dealer's 5 or 6. If you can't do these seemingly unorthodox moves, then maybe you should return to the more sedate form of blackjack that you are familiar with. Spanish 21 will sink you if you can't sail comfortably with the new Armada Play basic strategy. And if you want to actually show a profit at this new game, you are going to have to develop and successfully execute the Armada Ruse as a part of your playing strategy as well.

In conclusion, the combination of the Armada Play of the hands and the Armada Ruse, along with Armada Money Management principles, comprise the full *Armada Strategies for Spanish 21*. Use these techniques and they may help to make your future voyages against this game successful. Don't use them and you might be joining some of those heavy warships in the drink.

2

How the Game
is Played

The objective of any blackjack game is to beat the dealer. In Spanish 21, a secondary objective is also important—to go for the hand that gives the best possible return on your investment. Thus, there are some hands you will hit in Spanish 21 that you would never consider hitting at traditional blackjack because you are going for the premium rewards for certain designated hands. In general, however, the thrust of Spanish 21 is still to beat the dealer. You can beat the dealer by having a hand that is 21 or less that is higher than the dealer's hand, or it can be achieved by the dealer busting, which means the dealer going over 21. In Spanish 21, if the player and the dealer each have hands of 21, the player wins. This includes blackjacks, also known as naturals. If both the player and the dealer have a blackjack, the player is paid off at 3 to 2 (that means that for every two dollars you wagered you win three dollars). However, all other tied hands are considered pushes and neither the player nor the dealer wins.

Card Values

All cards have their face value. All picture cards are worth ten. All aces are worth either one or eleven, depending on how they are used. There are no 10-spot cards in the deck; therefore, in a six-deck game, there are 288 cards in the shoe, not 312 as in traditional blackjack. In this book, therefore, when I refer to 10 in the various strategies, I am referring to the *10-valued* cards of jack, queen, and king, but not the *10-spot* cards, which have been removed from the decks.

Hands where the ace can be used as either a one or 11 are called *soft hands*. All other hands are called *hard hands*. Thus A:2, A:3, and A:4 are respectively a *soft* 13, 14, and 15, while Q:3, J:4, K:5 are respectively a *hard* 13, 14, and 15. Multiple-card soft hands such as A:2,4 (soft 17) can be doubled and should be played based on the strategy for the soft total. Soft hands become hard hands when the ace must be valued as one or eleven, not both. If a player has an A:6 and receives a jack as his next card, the player now has a hard hand of 17. Some hands are referred to as "stiffs" because they tend to be long-range losers for the players. These hands include: 12, 13, 14, 15, and 16.

Procedures

Most Spanish 21 tables have spots for six or seven players. The dealer gives each player two cards and himself two cards. One of the dealer's cards is face up and the other is face down. In Spanish 21 games, the players' cards are usually dealt face up. Once all players have their two cards, they are faced with several strategy choices and options. We will judge each option and strategy decision from the perspective of the Armada Play basic strategy player to determine whether the option is good for the player, bad for the player, or sometimes good, sometimes bad, depending on how it is used.

Option # 1: The player can take a *hit*, which means to ask for another card. To do so in a multiple-deck Spanish 21 game, the player points to the hand and indicates a hit by tapping the table. You will note with interest that many players have developed their own style of pointing or calling for hits. Players may hit as many times as they desire—as long as they don't go over 21. The Armada Play basic strategy chart will tell you when hitting is the best option for a given hand against a given dealer upcard. [Group One Players please note that the play of many of the "stiff" hands is radically different from basic blackjack strategy and that some hands are hit in order to go for the bonuses.]

Option # 2: The player can *stand*, which means that he is satisfied with his hand and does not want any more cards. To stand, simply wave your hands over your cards to indicate "no more." The Armada Play basic strategy will tell you when standing is the best option for a given hand against a given dealer upcard. [Group One Players will note that you tend to stand on fewer hands than in traditional blackjack. That's because the dealer is much more likely to make good hands from certain stiff hands because of the diminution of 10-valued cards in the deck.]

Option # 3: The player can put up an extra bet *equal to* or *lower than* his original bet and *double down*. The player will then receive only one card on the hand. The player simply puts the bet next to his original bet. *A player may double down on any number of cards at Spanish 21.* This is an excellent option for the player who uses it properly according to the Armada Play basic strategy. [Group One Players: The doubling option is not used as frequently on the first two cards at Spanish 21 as it is with traditional blackjack because of the depleted decks.]

Option # 4: If a player receives a pair, he can opt to *split* them by putting up a bet that is equal to the original bet. The dealer will then deal the player a card on each hand and the player will play each hand separately. A pair of aces can only receive one card on each ace [Note: there might be some casinos that will allow more than one card on an ace.] but all other pairs may be hit as many times as the player wishes. *Players may split like-valued cards up to four times at Spanish 21.* This is called resplitting. Thus, if a player received a 2:2, split them and received another 2 on one or both of the 2s, he could resplit the new pairs. This is an excellent option for the player who uses it properly according to the Armada Play basic strategy.

Option # 5: Spanish 21 allows players to *double down after splitting* pairs. The procedure for this is the same as for doubling on the original cards. Once you split your pair and receive a second card on one of the splits, you may place an additional bet that is equal to or smaller than your original bet and indicate that you want to double. The dealer will then give you only one card. This is an excellent option for the player who uses it properly according to the Armada Play basic strategy. Again you can double on any number of cards after a split.

Option # 6: If the dealer has an ace showing, players can take *insurance* by placing a bet up to one-half the size of the original bet in the playing area marked *insurance.* This bet is a side bet that the dealer has a blackjack and is paid off at two to one. Insurance is not a good option for the Armada Play basic strategy player. [Insurance is not a good bet for the basic strategy player in traditional blackjack either, but it is an even worse bet in Spanish 21, again because of the reduction in the number of 10-valued cards in the deck.]

Option # 7: After you see your first two cards, Spanish 21 allows you to *surrender* your hand without playing it by giving up half your bet. However, if the dealer subsequently has a blackjack, you lose the entire bet. This is a good option for the player who uses it properly according to the Armada Play basic strategy.

Option # 8: Bonus hands receive special payouts as follows:
- a. Five-card 21 pays 3 to 2.
- b. Six-card 21 pays 2 to 1.
- c. Seven (or more)-card 21 pays 3 to 1.
- d. A three-card hand of 6-7-8 composed of mixed suits pays 3 to 2.
- e. A three-card hand of 6-7-8 composed of the same suit pays 2 to 1.
- f. A three-card hand of 6-7-8 composed of all spades pays 3 to 1.
- g. A 7-7-7 hand composed of mixed suits pays 3 to 2.
- h. A 7-7-7 hand composed of the same suit pays 2 to 1.
- i. A 7-7-7 hand composed of all spades pays 3 to 1.

Option # 9: A player may surrender the original bet but save the double-down bet. This rule does not apply if the hand is busted. This rule is called the Double-Down Rescue and is not a good option for the Armada Play basic strategy player. Ignore it.

Option # 10: There is a Jackpot bonus of $1,000 paid to any player who has 7-7-7 of the same suit if the dealer is also showing a seven (of any suit). When this occurs, all other players at the table receive a bonus of $50. Some casinos make the jackpot $1,000 per $5 wagered up to a maximum of $5,000 for a $25 or higher bet. This option will appeal to those players who like the idea that a bad run can be dramatically turned around with quick hit of luck.

The above options are common wherever Spanish 21 is played throughout the country. However, some casinos may also offer other options to their players, or limit the exercise of certain options. It is always wise to check the rules of the game you are about to play. If the casinos add options that simply reward certain hands without you having to take extra hits, or putting up side bets, then these are probably good for the player. However, be wary if the casinos add features to the existing game that call for you to put up extra money to receive a bonus. Such features usually come with a heavy price tag—a price that is paid by the player. Lastly, when the dealer has an Ace-6 (soft 17), he hits the hand which is a slightly unfavorable option for the players.

3

The Armada Play Basic Strategy

The basic strategy for Spanish 21 is much more complicated than the basic strategy for traditional blackjack because of the number of hands that require discrete choices based on the total number of cards in that hand. In order to make the Armada Play basic strategy for the play of the hands perfectly clear, I am going to approach it in two ways: First, I'll explain the play of every player hand against every dealer upcard. Then you'll find a chart which shows the same strategy in code. You can photocopy this chart and take it into the casino. Most casinos will allow you to use the Armada Play basic strategy chart, although you might want to memorize the Armada Play in order to use the Armada Ruse, which appears in chapter 7. Regardless of whether you photostat the strategy and bring it to the table, or memorize it, I believe it is still important to understand why you make the choices that you make at Spanish 21. You might find yourself playing at tables with players who are wary of the kinds of decisions that you're making. With confidence you can ignore their advice and stick to the Armada Play basic strategy.

Hard Hands

You will receive many more poor or stiff hands at Spanish 21 than you will at traditional 21 because of the removal of the 10-spots from play. This means that you will hit these hands more often than in traditional blackjack as well. Keep in mind that you can double on any number of cards so a hand of 11 made with three cards versus a dealer's 6 is an occasion to double down. Please note the times when you must abandon a conservative strategy to go for the special premium bonus hands. Do not hesitate to try for the bonuses when indicated, otherwise your monetary expectation will not be as positive. Once again note that the designation 10 means the 10-valued cards jack, queen, and king, not the 10-spot cards.

The best way to memorize the following strategy is to take each discreet player hand and memorize one a day for a month, or two a day for half a month. Such a memorization schedule would not be daunting to the average player. In fact, some of the hands such as 19, 20, 21 are no brainers.

Player hand of 5 through 8: Hit against all dealer upcards.

Player hand of 9: Hit against all dealer upcards except:
    1. Double down against dealer's 6 when player has two-card 9.
    2. Hit when the player has a three-card 9.

Player hand of 10: Hit against a dealer's 8, 9, 10, ace. Double down against a dealer's 2, 3, 4, 5, 6 or 7 except:
    1. Hit with five or more cards against a dealer's 2 or 3.
    2. Hit with six cards against a dealer's 4.
    3. Hit with four or more cards against a dealer's 7.

Player hand of 11: Hit against a dealer's 9, 10 or ace. Double down against a dealer's 2, 3, 4, 5, 6, 7, or 8 except:
    1. Hit with four or more cards against a dealer's 2, 7, or 8.
    2. Hit with five or more cards against a dealer's 3, 4, 5, or 6.

Player hand of 12: Hit against all dealer upcards.

Player hand of 13: Hit against dealer's 2, 3, 4, 7, 8, 9, 10 or ace. Stand against a dealer's 5 or 6 except:
    1. Hit with five or more cards against a dealer's 5.
    2. Hit with four or more cards against a dealer's 6.

Player hand of 14: Hit against dealer's 2, 3, 7, 8, 9, 10 or ace. Stand against a dealer's 4, 5, or 6 except:
   1. Hit with four or more cards against a dealer's 4.
   2. Hit with five or more cards against the dealer's 5 or 6.

Player hand of 15: Hit against dealer's 7, 8, 9 10 or ace. Stand against dealer's 2 through 6 except:
   1. Hit with four or more cards against a dealer's 2.
   2. Hit with five or more cards against a dealer's 3 or 4.
   3. Hit with six cards against a dealer's 5 or 6.

Player hand of 16: Hit against a dealer's 7, 8, 9, 10. Surrender against a dealer's ace. Stand against a dealer's 2 through 6 except:
   1. Hit with five or more cards against a dealer's 2.
   2. Hit with six cards against a dealer's 3 or 4.

Player hand of 17: Stand against all dealer upcards except:
   1. Surrender against a dealer's ace.
   2. Hit with six cards against a dealer's 8, 9 or 10.

Player hand of 18: Stand against all dealer upcards.

Player hand of 19: Stand against all dealer upcards.

Player hand of 20: Stand against all dealer upcards.

Player hand of 21: Stand against all dealer upcards.

Soft Hands

Again, soft hands are any hands where the ace can be used as one or eleven. An important thing to keep in mind is the fact that you can double on any number of cards in Spanish 21. Soft hands with more than two cards are prime candidates for possible doubling. You could begin a hand with an ace-2 (soft 13), hit it, receive a 4, and now you have a soft 17 (ace-2-4). You would then follow the Armada Play basic strategy for soft 17 in that case.

Player hand of soft 13: Hit against all dealer upcards.

Player hand of soft 14: Hit against all dealer upcards.

Player hand of soft 15: Hit against all dealer upcards.

Player hand of soft 16: Double down against a dealer's 6. Hit against all other dealer upcards except:
> 1. Hit with four or more cards against a dealer's 6.

Player hand of soft 17: Hit against a dealer's 2, 3, 7, 8, 9, 10, ace. Double down against a dealer's 4, 5, or 6 except:
> 1. Hit with three or more cards against a dealer's 4.
> 2. Hit with four or more cards against a dealer's 5.
> 3. Hit with five or more cards against a dealer's 6.

Player hand of soft 18: Stand against a dealer's 2, 3, 7 or 8. Double down against a dealer's 4, 5, or 6. Hit against a dealer's 9, 10 or ace except:
> 1. Hit with four or more cards against a dealer's 2, 3, 4 or 8.
> 2. Hit with five or more cards against a dealer's 5.
> 3. Hit with six cards against a dealer's 6.

Player hand of soft 19, 20, 21: Stand against all dealer upcards.

Pairs

When you split pairs, you play each end of the split based on the Armada Play basic strategy for that hand. Thus, if you split 2,2 and receive a 9 on one 2 and an 8 on the other 2, you would follow the strategy for hard 11 and hard 10 respectively.

Player hand of 2,2: Hit against a dealer's 2, 8, 9, 10, or ace. Split against a dealer's 3, 4, 5, 6, or 7.

Player hand of 3,3: Hit against a dealer's 2, 8, 9, 10, or ace. Split against a dealer's 3, 4, 5, 6, or 7.

Player hand of 4,4: Hit against all dealer upcards.

Player hand of 5,5: Double down against a dealer's 2, 3, 4, 5, 6, or 7. Hit against a dealer's 8, 9, 10, or ace.

Player hand of 6,6: Hit against a dealer's 2, 3, 7, 8, 9, 10, or ace. Split against a dealer's 4, 5, or 6.

Player hand of 7,7: Split against a dealer's 2, 3, 4, 5, 6, or 7. Hit against a dealer's 8, 9, 10, or ace.

Player hand of 8,8: Split against a dealer's hand of 2, 3, 4, 5, 6, 7, 8, 9, or 10. Surrender against a dealer's ace.

Player hand of 9,9: Stand against a dealer 2, 7, 10, or ace. Split against a dealer's 3, 4, 5, 6, 8, or 9.

Player hand of 10,10: Stand against all dealer upcards.

Player hand of A,A: Split against all dealer upcards.

Armada Play basic strategy players never use the Double-Down Rescue option or the Insurance option as these are options that favor the house. With proper Armada Play, the casino will have an 0.82 percent edge over the player. For a player playing 60 hands an hour (see chapter 7), this translates into a deficit of less than one bet every two hours. It doesn't get much better than this in casino games. As the lyrics to a *My Fair Lady* song go: "With a little bit of luck you won't get hurt!" In truth, Spanish 21 can offer the Armada Play basic strategy player a game where "a little bit of luck" is all that is necessary to come out ahead. Attached to the Armada Ruse it might even give you an edge!

Frank Scoblete's Armada Play Basic Strategy for Spanish 21

H = hit; D = double; Sur = surrender; S = stand; X = split;
Sh = stand except hit on total number of cards indicated
Dh = double except hit on total number of cards indicated

					Dealer's Upcard					
Hard:	2	3	4	5	6	7	8	9	10	Ace
5-8	H	H	H	H	H	H	H	H	H	H
9	H	H	H	H	Dh3+	H	H	H	H	H
10	Dh5+	Dh5+	Dh6	D	D	Dh4+	H	H	H	H
11	Dh4+	Dh5+	Dh5+	Dh5+	Dh5+	Dh4+	Dh4+	H	H	H
12	H	H	H	H	H	H	H	H	H	H
13	H	H	H	Sh5+	Sh4+	H	H	H	H	H
14	H	H	Sh4+	Sh5+	Sh5+	H	H	H	H	H
15	Sh4+	Sh5+	Sh5+	Sh6	Sh6	H	H	H	H	H
16	Sh5+	Sh6	Sh6	S	S	H	H	H	H	Sur
17	S	S	S	S	S	S	Sh6	Sh6	Sh6	Sur
18	S	S	S	S	S	S	S	S	S	S
19	S	S	S	S	S	S	S	S	S	S
20	S	S	S	S	S	S	S	S	S	S
21	S	S	S	S	S	S	S	S	S	S
Soft	2	3	4	5	6	7	8	9	10	Ace
13	H	H	H	H	H	H	H	H	H	H
14	H	H	H	H	H	H	H	H	H	H
15	H	H	H	H	H	H	H	H	H	H
16	H	H	H	H	Dh4+	H	H	H	H	H
17	H	H	Dh3+	Dh4+	Dh5+	H	H	H	H	H
18	Sh4+	Sh4+	Dh4+	Dh5+	Dh6	S	Sh4+	H	H	H
19	S	S	S	S	S	S	S	S	S	S
20	S	S	S	S	S	S	S	S	S	S
21	S	S	S	S	S	S	S	S	S	S
Pairs	2	3	4	5	6	7	8	9	10	Ace
A:A	X	X	X	X	X	X	X	X	X	X
2:2	H	X	X	X	X	X	H	H	H	H
3:3	H	X	X	X	X	X	H	H	H	H
4:4	H	H	H	H	H	H	H	H	H	H
5:5	D	D	D	D	D	D	H	H	H	H
6:6	H	H	X	X	X	H	H	H	H	H
7:7	X	X	X	X	X	X	H	H	H	H
8:8	X	X	X	X	X	X	X	X	X	Sur
9:9	S	X	X	X	X	S	X	X	S	S
10:10	S	S	S	S	S	S	S	S	S	S

4

Everything You Want to Know About Spanish 21

When I first started researching Spanish 21, I had many questions concerning the game. My first impulse was to dismiss it as another attempt by casinos to gouge the players. After all, removing the 10-spot cards from the deck would increase the house edge over the basic strategy player to almost 3 percent. However, when I realized that the bonus hands and special rules were quite favorable to the player, I had to reevaluate that first impulse. Knowing now that the casino has only a reasonable 0.82 percent edge with the Armada Play basic strategy, makes Spanish 21—in the great casino scheme of things—rank right up there with the very best of games. That is not to say, however, that Spanish 21 can rival regular blackjack. Remember that that 0.82 percent house edge, while comparing favorably with almost all other casino games does not quite stack up favorably with regular blackjack. The following list will give you the *approximate* casino edges for various games of blackjack depending on the number of decks in use and the rules variations. It will give you a good idea of where Spanish 21 fits in. The assumption for the chart is that the player is using the appropriate basic strategy for the games. Obviously, the edges for each game can go up or down depending on the rules in effect.

Game	Casino Edge
regular single deck	0 to +or −0.10 percent
double exposure multiple decks*	.30 to 1.00 percent
regular two decks	.35 percent
regular four decks	.52 percent
regular six decks	.58 percent
regular eight decks	.61 percent
Spanish 21 six decks	.82 percent

*requires a different basic strategy for play of the hands

How Spanish 21 Compares with other Games

Here is a general view of how Spanish 21 stacks up against all casino games other than regular blackjack. This chart gives you a clear picture of just how good a game Spanish 21 really is.

Since some games have various bets, I have divided the chart not only by game but by bets in the various games. I have included card counting on the list and I shall deal with the issue of counting cards at Spanish 21 in a separate chapter. Keep in mind that while some games might look fairly good in their house edges there are other factors to consider including the size of the bankroll required to effectively play the "betting style" and the speed of the game. For example, while the banking of Pai Gow Poker looks as if it might yield a positive result, the monumental bankroll required to bank every hand (not to mention whether the casino will allow one player to bank every hand) precludes this bet for any but the most wealthy players. All edges on this chart are approximate. For craps bets with odds, the don't pass and don't come bets actually have fractionally lower house edges than indicated.

Game	Betting Style	House Edge
Blackjack	card counting	.5% to 1.5%*
Pai Gow poker	bank	.5 % *
Single-deck blackjack	basic strategy	0% to .10%
Craps	pass/come/don't pass/don't come 100X odds	.02%
Craps	pass/come/don't pass/don't come 20X odds	.10%
Craps	pass/come/don't pass/don't come 10X odds	.18%
Double exposure blackjack	basic strategy	.30%
Craps	pass/come/don't pass/don't come 5X odds	.33%
Double-deck blackjack	basic strategy	.35%
Craps	pass/come/don't pass/don't come 3X odds	.47%
Four-deck blackjack	basic strategy	.52%
Six-deck blackjack	basic strategy	.58 %
Eight-deck blackjack	basic strategy	.61%
Craps	pass/come/don't pass/don't come 2X odds	.61%
Baccarat	bank with 4% commission	.67%
Spanish 21	Armada Play Strategy	.82%
Craps	pass/come/don't pass/don't come 1X odds	.85%
Baccarat	bank with 5% commission	1.17%
Roulette single-zero wheel	outside bets with surrender	1.35%
Baccarat	player	1.36%
Craps	pass/come/don't pass/don't come no odds	1.41%
Craps	place the 6 and 8	1.52%
Craps	don't place 6 or 8	1.82%
Three-Card poker	Bold Card Play Strategy ante and play	2.14%
Three Card poker	pair plus	2.32%
Craps	lay 4 or 10	2.44%
Pai Gow poker	player	2.5%
Craps	buy 4 or 10 for $39	2.5%
Craps	don't place 5 or 9	2.5%
Craps	buy 5 or 9 for $38	2.56%
Roulette double-zero wheel	outside bets with surrender	2.63%
Roulette single-zero wheel	all bets	2.7%
Craps	buy 4 or 10 for $35	2.78%
Let It Ride	Bold Card Play Strategy	2.8%
Sic Bo	small or big	2.8%
Craps	don't place 4 or 10	3.03%
Craps	buy the 4 or 10 for $30	3.23%
Craps	lay 5 or 9	3.23%
Red Dog	basic strategy	3.5%
Craps	buy 4 or 10 for $25	3.85%
Craps	lay 6 or 8	4.0%
Craps	place the 5 or 9	4.0%
Craps	buy the 4 or 10 for $20	4.76%
Roulette double-zero wheel	all bets	5.26%
Caribbean Stud	Bold Card Play Strategy	5.3%
Crapless craps	pass/come no odds	5.38%
Craps	field	5.55%
Craps	place the 4 or 10	6.67%
Roulette double-zero wheel	five number bet	7.89%
Craps	hard 6 or 8; Big 6 or 8	9.09%
Sic Bo	all other bets range	9.7% to 48%
Big Wheel	bets range from	11% to 24%
Craps	hard 4 or 10	11.11%
Craps	3, 11, any craps	11.11%
Craps	2, 12, or hopping hardways	13.89%
Baccarat	tie	14.1%
Craps	any 7; over/under 7	16.67%
Keno	various wagers	25%

* for player

Any Questions?

The following are the most frequently asked questions concerning Spanish 21. I would like to thank blackjack expert Fred Renzey, author of the previously mentioned *Blackjack Bluebook* and editor of the excellent monthly newsletter *The Blackjack Mentor,* for working out much of the math and computer simulations for Spanish 21. In some cases, Fred's analysis is a "best estimate" and not an exact calculation. However, when dealing with (give-or-take) tenths of a percent, the answers are sufficiently accurate to give you a good basis for judgment.

How often will I get a blackjack at Spanish 21?

Spanish 21 differs from regular blackjack in many ways, not the least of which is in the frequency of certain situations arising. One of the key variables in blackjack favorability has to do with the 3 to 2 payoff on a natural 21. Without that 3 to 2 payout the casino would have a much greater edge. Anything that reduces the number of blackjacks that a player can get, reduces that player's overall expectation. However, while Spanish 21 does offer a nice perk when both the player and the dealer have a blackjack (the player wins), such an eventuality does not occur all that often. Instead, the total reduction in the number of blackjacks at Spanish 21 has helped the casino considerably. In regular six-deck blackjack, you can expect to see a blackjack approximately once every 21 hands. In Spanish 21, you can expect to see a blackjack approximately once every 24 hands.

What are the chances of a dealer busting when he has various upcards at Spanish 21 as compared to regular blackjack?

The late Lenny Frome worked out the comparative bust rates in his excellent booklet *Expert Strategy for Spanish 21* (Compu-Flyers, 2025 S. Eastern Ave., Las Vegas, NV 89119) for the various starting dealer hands.

Dealer's Upcard	Bust Rate Spanish 21	Bust Rate Regular BJ
2	31.6%	36.1%
3	33.8%	37.2%
4	36.2%	39.8%
5	37.9%	42.3%
6	40.6%	44.6%
7	26.7%	26.7%
8	24.8%	24.3%
9	22.7%	22.6%
10	21.1%	21.0%
Ace	14.0%	12.8%

Therefore, the overall bust rate for Spanish 21 is 27.6 percent while the total bust rate for regular blackjack is 28.5 percent. Why does the dealer bust less often (with the single exception of an upcard of 7) at Spanish 21 than at regular blackjack? Simple: fewer 10-valued cards to send him over 21.

Isn't it true that when you double down, you want to get a 10-valued card? How does Spanish 21 stack up against regular blackjack in receiving a ten on a double down?

When you double on an 11, you do want to get a 10 card. When you double on 9 or 10, you want an ace first and a 10 if chance won't give you the ace. However, desiring a 10 every time you double down is not the way to go. When you double on soft hands, you usually want the card that can give you a total or 20 or 21. For example, if you double on A:6, then you would love to get a 4 or a 3 and not a 10 because a 4 brings your total to 21 while a 3 will bring it to 20. Still, hard doubles of 9, 10 or 11 occur more often than soft doubles so the absence of 10s does hurt the player's expectation since he will not double down as often in Spanish 21 as he will in regular blackjack. In Spanish 21, you will receive a 10-valued card once every four hands as compared with regular blackjack where you will receive a 10-valued card once every 3.2 hands.

How often will I be dealt any of the bonus hands such as 6-7-8 or 7-7-7 or 7-7-7 of spades? How does the respective rates of receiving these hands differ from regular blackjack? How helpful are these hands to my overall expectation.

Here are the comparisons you asked for:

Hand	Regular 6-Deck Blackjack	Spanish 21
6-7-8 mixed suits	once in 363 hands	once in 285 hands
6-7-8 same suit	once in 5,802 hands	once in 4,560 hands
6-7-8 spades	once in 23,210 hands	once in 18,240 hands
7-7-7 mixed suits	once in 2,477 hands	once in 1,947 hands
7-7-7 same suit	once in 62,667 hands	once in 49,249 hands
7-7-7 spades	once in 250,666 hands	once in 196,977 hands

Because of the infrequency of the bonus hands, their overall effect on your expectation is limited. If we assume 80 hands in an hour of play, you can expect to play 320 hands per four hours of play. I use four hours of play as a standard because the casinos usually use four hours as a guideline for comping purposes. You will therefore receive slightly more than one bonus hand for every four hours of play if you take into consideration all the possible bonus hands that you can receive. Of course, the hand that you will get the most is 6-7-8 of mixed suits which pays 3 to 2. It's the equivalent of getting an extra blackjack for every four hours of play. Sound good? Read the next paragraph.

Here's another way to look at these figures. If regular six-deck blackjack gives us one natural in 21 hands, we can extrapolate that we'll receive slightly less than 4 blackjacks per 80 hands (or 4 per hour) and slightly more than 15 blackjacks in 4 hours of play. Now, in Spanish 21 we'll get only 1 blackjack in 24 hands, which translates into slightly more than 13 blackjacks in 4 hours. If we add the bonus of one hand per four hours at a payout of 3 to 2 (an extra blackjack in concept), we can see that at the end of 4 hours of play at Spanish 21, we are down 1 blackjack. The addition of the bonus does not make up for the subtraction of the 10s, which has led to a diminishing of the total number of blackjacks that we receive. Therein lies one of the reasons that the casino has an extra edge at Spanish 21.

So the answer to the question concerning how helpful these bonus hands are to your expectation is: not that helpful when all is said and done.

Why does Spanish 21 have a lower expectation than regular blackjack with all those great bonuses?

If you add all the bonuses together at Spanish 21, they cannot make up for the devastating effects of removing the 10-spot cards from the deck. In addition to getting one blackjack *payout* fewer per 4 hours as in the example above, you will not have as many opportunities to double down as you would in regular blackjack. Those double-down opportunities at regular blackjack increase your wins or lower your losses on the hands indicated. Thus, in six decks, instead of facing a .52 percent edge, you face a slightly greater .82 percent edge. That extra .30 percent is the result of the subtraction of the 10s and the addition of the bonuses.

However, it is in the area of card counting—the one tried-and-true way for a player to actually get a slight mathematical edge over the casinos—that we see the genius behind the invention of the game of Spanish 21. This we'll see in the next chapter.

If Spanish 21 is not as good as regular blackjack why is it gaining in popularity?

First of all when you compare Spanish 21 to regular blackjack, the deficit of .30 in terms of the house edge for the Armada Strategy as opposed to the basic strategy in regular blackjack should be put into two contexts—mathematical and emotional. In terms of math, a house edge of .52 percent means that you will lose approximately 52 cents for every $100 that you wager in the long run at regular blackjack. This assumes, of course, that you are playing the proper basic strategy. At Spanish 21, you will lose 82 cents per $100 wagered in the long run. That's a difference of 30 cents.

Let's translate that into hours played to really get an idea of the impact of a .30 difference in expectation between the two games. If we use 80 hands an hour as our guideline, let us see what the expectation is for various levels of betting at regular six-deck blackjack as opposed to Spanish 21.

Betting Level	Expected loss per 4 hrs of play at Spanish 21	Expected loss per 4 hrs of play at Regular Six-Deck BJ
$5 per hand	$13.12	$8.32
$10 per hand	$26.24	$16.64
$15 per hand	$39.36	$24.96
$25 per hand	$65.60	$41.60
$50 per hand	$131.20	$83.20
$100 per hand	$262.40	$166.40

Here's another way to read the above chart. The Armada Strategy player at Spanish 21 can expect to lose approximately two-and-a-half bets more than he wins per four hours, while the basic strategy player at blackjack will lose only one-and-a-half bets more than he wins in the same time. Essentially, you lose one more bet per four hours at play at Spanish 21 than you do at regular blackjack. That bet is, metaphorically speaking, the loss of the extra blackjack I discussed previously! You will have to decide if the loss of one bet more or less is worth worrying about.

As to why the game of Spanish 21 is gaining in popularity, that is due to the emotional factors. The game seemingly offers more decisions for the players in addition to rules and options that are unheard of in regular blackjack such as doubling on any number of cards. The game has a high excitement level according to the players who play it. Despite the fact that the above chart clearly shows the monetary impact of a difference of just .30 percent between Spanish 21 and regular blackjack, Spanish 21's emotional underpinnings are more pleasing to the average player.

In regular blackjack many players find themselves irritated by the play of other players at their tables. This is not yet a demonstrable factor at Spanish 21 as very few people know of the Armada Play basic strategy for playing the game. Thus, the overwhelming majority of players are groping for their decisions and very few of them feel strongly enough about their own individual strategies to bug other players about *their* strategies, as is constantly done at regular blackjack. My own experience has shown me that there is much more of a "party" atmosphere at Spanish 21 than there is at regular blackjack. It's a fun game, there's no denying it.

Much of the fun comes from anticipating possibly big payoffs—something just about all gamblers fantasize about. Casinos cater to dreams and fantasies, after all, and Spanish 21 supplies these in spades...literally.

But there is a rub. As more and more people discover how to play the game, and as more and more people employ the Armada Play basic strategy for the play of their hands, players might find those obnoxious busybodies appearing at Spanish 21 as well. Only time will tell.

How many differences in basic strategy are there between regular blackjack and Spanish 21?

There are fifty-three strategy differences between regular basic strategy for multiple-deck games and The Armada Play basic strategy for Spanish 21. In making this comparison, I have used a regulation six-deck blackjack game that allows doubling on any first two cards, doubling after splits, resplits up to four hands, where the dealer hits on soft 17 and surrender is allowed.

Dealer Upcard	Player Hand	Basic Strategy Regular 6-Deck	Armada Strategy
2	hard 13	stand	hit
	hard 14	stand	hit
	hard 15	stand	stand/hit 4+
	hard 16	stand	stand/hit 5+
	soft 18	stand	stand/hit 4+
	2:2	split	stand
	3:3	split	stand
3	hard 9	double	hit
	hard 13	stand	hit
	hard 14	stand	hit
	hard 15	stand	stand/hit 5+
	hard 16	stand	stand/hit 6
	soft 17	double	hit
	soft 18	double	stand/hit 4+
	6:6	split	hit

Dealer Upcard	Player Hand	Basic Strategy Regular 6-Deck	Armada Strategy
4	hard 9	double	hit
	hard 12	stand	hit
	hard 13	stand	hit
	hard 14	stand	stand/hit 4+
	hard 15	stand	stand/hit 5+
	hard 16	stand	stand/hit 6
	soft 16	double	hit
5	hard 9	double	hit
	hard 12	stand	hit
	hard 13	stand	stand/hit 5+
	hard 14	stand	stand/hit 5+
	hard 15	stand	stand/hit 6
	soft 13	double	hit
	soft 14	double	hit
	soft 15	double	hit
	soft 16	double	hit
	4:4	split	hit
6	hard 12	stand	hit
	hard 13	stand	stand/hit 4+
	hard 14	stand	stand/hit 5+
	hard 15	stand	stand/hit 6
	soft 13	double	hit
	soft 14	double	hit
	soft 15	double	hit
	4:4	split	stand
7	-----	-------	--------
8	hard 10	double	hit
	hard 17	stand	stand/hit 6
	soft 18	stand	stand/hit 4+
9	hard 10	double	hit
	hard 11	double	hit
	hard 16	surrender	hit
	hard 17	stand	stand/hit 6
10	hard 11	double	hit
	hard 15	surrender	hit
	hard 16	surrender	hit
	hard 17	stand	stand/hit 6
Ace	hard 11	double	hit
	hard 17	stand	surrender

What are the total number of initial two-card player's hands in regular six-deck blackjack as opposed to Spanish 21?

The total number of initial two card hands at regular six deck blackjack is 48,516. The total number of hands in Spanish 21 is 41,328.

What are the total and relative frequencies of initial two-card player hands for hands with aces and 10-valued cards, and hands with pairs?

Hand	Total Frequency Regular 6-Deck	Total Frequency Spanish 21
A-10	2,304 1 in 21 hands	1,728 1 in 24 hands
A-9 (8, 7, etc.)	576 1 in 84 hands	576 1 in 72 hands
A-A	276 1 in 176 hands	276 1 in 150 hands
10-10	4,560 1 in 11 hands	5,112 1 in 16 hands
10-9 (8, 7, etc.)	2,304 1 in 21 hands	1,728 1 in 24 hands
9:9 (8:8, etc.)	276 1 in 176 hands	276 1 in 150 hands

5

Card Counting at Spanish 21

Whenever I tell people at my public lectures that the best way to get an edge over the casinos is to count cards at blackjack, I am inevitably asked one, a few or all of the following questions:

"But isn't it hard to do?"

"Don't you have to have a photographic memory to do that?"

"How can you possibly memorize every card that comes out of a deck or a shoe?"

"Isn't it illegal to count cards?"

"Don't you have to be good at math to do that?"

My answer to all those questions has that billy-goat ring to it: Nah!

While counting cards is not the equivalent of, say, counting your blessings, it is not that much more difficult. Technically, it is as easy as one, two, three.

One: You must be able to add simple numbers.

Two: You must be able to subtract simple numbers.

Three: You must be able to divide simple numbers.

If you made it past the fifth grade, you have the necessary intellectual skills to become a card counter. But (isn't there always a "but" to anything that seems easy?) you must have certain personality traits that are not as easy to find: discipline, concentration, and a burning desire to beat the casinos. You must also have a fairly strong emotional constitution to weather the swings of fortune that inevitably occur to even the best counters.

Card counting, developed by Edward O. Thorp in the early 1960s, refined by a host of researchers and players/writers ever since, is the most devastating *legal* technique ever developed to beat the casinos at their own games. It is no lie that casinos sweat out the blackjack action because they know that some players can beat them consistently. It's also no lie that in places such as Nevada card counters are routinely asked to leave the blackjack pits because they're "too good." (On a personal note, having experience the "we don't want your action here because you're too good" routine, I can say this: No American citizen should be told by an American business that his action and/or his person isn't wanted. It's wrong when a restaurant does it to a person of a given skin color; it's wrong when a casino does it to a person with a given talent!) Thankfully, Atlantic City doesn't ban card counters and some Atlantic City casinos still offer games that can be beaten by skilled players—games with good rules and, more importantly, games with deep penetration. At least they do as I write this.

But I'm getting ahead of myself.

Although much research has been done into card counting and the esoterica of skilled play, the actual practice of card counting can be learned in the space of a few minutes and it is absolutely unnecessary to have any arcane knowledge to put it into play or to become proficient at it. You don't have to know the physics and chemistry of the automobile to get in, turn the key, and drive like hell. So too with card counting.

What you need to know is also as easy as one, two, three:

One: You need a card counting method that you can apply comfortably in a casino.

Two: You need some variations in the basic strategy to increase your chances of winning when the game favors you or decrease your losses when it favors the casino.

Three: You need a bet-sizing scheme that exploits favorable opportunities.

There are many good card-counting systems on the market (and a few lousy ones) from which to choose. Some of them are called "advanced systems" or "multiparameter systems" or "multilevel systems" and some are called "simple systems" or "level one" systems. They all do essentially the same thing. They keep track of the relationship of small cards (2,3,4,5,6,7) to big cards (9,10, Ace) in the remaining decks. Some are balanced counts that keep track of the same number of small cards as high cards. Some are unbalanced counts that count a disproportionate number of the small cards as compared to big cards. Some systems keep track of every card; some keep track of most cards; and still others keep track of select cards. I did a complete analysis of most legitimate card-counting systems for my book *Best Blackjack* and found that the difference between a simple level-one count and the most advanced *practical* count was not worth the extra effort and fatigue to get the slightly better edge that the more advanced systems could give. By way of analogy, the simple level-one system I now use (after trying some of the more complicated multilevel systems earlier in my career) is the equivalent of hitting a home run to right or left centerfield, while the multilevel, multiparameter counts were like hitting a home run over the centerfield fence.

So the system that I now use and have been using for the past eight years or so is simple and easy to play. It's called the Hi-Lo (sometimes High-Low) and was developed by Julian Braun (yes the same Julian Braun who worked on Spanish 21) and perfected by Stanford Wong, two great blackjack theorists.

Card counting is based on the documented fact that high cards favor the player and low cards favor the casino. When more high cards remain in the shoe, the player has the edge. When more small cards remain in the shoe, the casino has the edge. A card counting system keeps track of the relationship of high to low cards in order to decide when it is appropriate to increase one's bet. You want to bet higher amounts when the counts favor you (called "high counts" or "positive counts") and you want to bet lower amounts—or no amounts—when the count favors the casino (called "low counts" or "negative counts").

To do this, the Hi-Lo count assigns the following values to the cards:

2 = +1	7 = 0	10 = -1
3 = +1	8 = 0	J = -1
4 = +1	9 = 0	Q = -1
5 = +1		K = -1
6 = +1		A = -1

When you start off, the count is neutral. Unfortunately, a neutral count in six-deck games does not mean that the game is even. It means the casino has an approximately 0.5 percent edge. As cards come out of the shoe, you add or subtract. Thus, if the first cards to come out are a ten, jack, and queen, the count is now -3. The shoe is beginning to favor the casino even more. However, if the first cards coming out are 2, 4, 5, 6 then the count is +4 and the shoe is slowly moving in the direction of the player. Again, as cards come out of the shoe, you add or subtract depending on what those cards are. This is called keeping track of the *running count*.

At what counts will a six-deck shoe actually favor the player—that is, give the player an advantage over the casino? To find this out you must use your division skills (see, getting past fifth grade was important!). You must estimate how many decks have been played and divide the remaining decks in the shoe into your count. This is called establishing the *true count*. Let us say that two decks have been played in a six-deck shoe. That means that four decks remain to be played. Let us also say that your running count is +12. Divide four into 12 and you now have a true count of +3. What does that mean in terms of a player or casino edge? It means the player has an edge of approximately 1 percent over the casino at this point because every point in the true count is approximately the equivalent of a 0.5 percent! (You start with a -0.5, add to that +1.5 which equals +1.)

Simple as one, two, three.

Let's review:

One: Find the running count = addition and subtraction!

Two: Find the true count = division!

Three: Find the percentage edge = division, addition and subtraction from the original casino edge of 0.5 percent!

To actually take advantage of your knowledge and win money, the next step requires you to increase your bets when the edge favors you. This next skill is often the thing that destroys would-be counters, as they misunderstand what an edge of 1 percent (or 2 or 3 percent) really means. Rather than tell you what it really means, let me tell you what a 1, 2 or 3 percent edge *doesn't mean*. It *doesn't mean* you are definitely going to win! So when you increase your bets in these favorable situations, you must not increase them to the point where a losing streak will wipe out your bankroll. Many a would-be card counter can probably be found outside a casino mumbling to himself: "But I had the edge! How come I'm broke?" As a rule of thumb the total amount of money you should have to back your card counting at blackjack should be between 100 to 200 times your *maximum* bet. So if you intend to bet $10 in neutral and low counts but $80 in high counts, you should have between $8,000 and $16,000 behind you.

Finally, you might want to make some changes in your basic strategy decisions based on the count. The following are common basic strategy changes based on the *true count* that will also help you get the edge in a regular blackjack game:

-2 or less = smallest bet possible or sit out

-1 or less = hit 13 against the dealer's 2 or 3

          = hit 12 against a dealer's 4

     0 = stand on 16 with three or more cards vs. dealer's 10

+1 or more = double 9 vs. dealer's 2

+2 or more = stand on 12 against the dealer's 2 or 3

          = double on 8 vs. dealer's 6

+3 or more = insure all hands against a dealer's ace

          = double 10 vs. dealer's ace

          = double 8 vs. dealer's 5

The above is an accurate albeit concise primer on six-deck card counting at regular blackjack where the dealer hits soft 17. Now to the question of card counting at Spanish 21.

We have already seen where the Armada Play basic strategy player at Spanish 21 ranks with the basic strategy player at regular blackjack—not a huge difference as compared with the wide edges on most casino games. We have also seen how the game compares to all other games and various bets at those games. In the latter perspective, the game is one of the best offerings on the casino floor. As we have seen, card counting at regular blackjack takes what is essentially a slight edge for the casino and gives it to the player. A card counter can get between a 0.5 and a 1.5 percent edge over the casino, depending on what games he plays and his skill level. Since the composition of the decks remaining to be played (and thus the advantage at the game) is constantly shifting from player to house and back again, a good card counter knows when the composition of the remaining cards favors him or when it favors the house. Are there relatively more aces and tens remaining to be played? The edge now favors the player. Are there more small cards (2, 3, 4, 5, 6) left in the deck or shoe? The game now favors the casino. As we have seen, the player achieves his overall edge at regular blackjack by betting more when the remaining cards favor him and betting less when they don't.

Counting cards at Spanish 21 presented some interesting dilemmas, not the least of which was which counting system would work best against the game. I asked blackjack expert Fred Renzey to help me develop a card counting system that would be effective against Spanish 21. Before we could do so, we had several questions that needed to be answered.

Here were our initial questions:

1. Since many of the premium hands such as five, six and seven-card 21s, along with certain options such as doubling on any number of cards, would work best when the count is low (the count is low most of the time during a Spanish 21 game since there are no 10-spot cards), we thought they would not be as significant a factor when the count was neutral (an equal number of high and low cards) or in the player's favor. Therefore as the count started to creep up to favorability, would the bonus hands become less frequent taking whatever

favorable impact they originally had? The answer was yes. But the big question we had was this: Would we see a *count reversal* in extremely low counts, when the deck was heavily depleted of the 10-valued cards because the bonus hands would become *more* frequent? The answer was that we didn't. The bonus hands, even in *extremely* low counts, just didn't hit often enough to help the player's negative expectations. In short, when the count went down—bonus hands or no bonus hands—the player faced even bigger house edges.

2. The second area of questioning had to do with the helpfulness of the rules concerning blackjack ties—the player wins them—in neutral and favorable decks. The fact is player and dealer ties with blackjacks occur so infrequently in neutral counts and even less frequently in the low counts that pervade Spanish 21, that the rule has only negligible positive impact on the overall player expectation. Nowhere is this more graphically shown than in the insurance option. In regular blackjack, there are times when taking insurance is a wise move for a card counter. When the true count reaches plus 3 or more, that's the time for insuring any hand you have against the dealer's upcard of ace. In a regular six-deck game, you can expect to have a favorable insurance bet approximately once in every 160 hands or twice every 4 hours if we are playing 80 hands per hour. In Spanish 21, we will encounter the good insurance moment approximately once in every 2,500 hands! That's once every 30 hours! At 4 hours of play per day, you will get a favorable insurance bet once every 8 days! A favorable insurance moment that occurs once every 30 hours doesn't make much of a dent in the overall negativity of the Spanish 21 game as does a favorable insurance bet once every two hours at regular blackjack.

3. The third area of questioning had to do with the strength of the casino's .82 percent edge. How solidly in place was it compared with regular blackjack? Would this edge be much, much tougher to overcome than the .52 percent edge at normal blackjack? For example, in *independent* trial games whatever the initial house edge is—well, that's what the house

edge is. The percentages can't be changed. A perfectly balanced double-zero roulette wheel will yield a house edge of 5.26 percent and, short of putting glue in the pockets, there is nothing a player can do to change this fact. However, because of the nature of *dependent* trial games—the edge actually does change from hand to hand. The questions are: How often does the house edge change? Does it ever change to benefit the player at times? And are these times enough to beat the game in the long run?

What we found was that the Spanish 21 edge for the house was almost—though not quite—an immovable object. The Spanish 21 edge of .82 percent was much tougher to overcome than the .52 percent edge in a regular six-deck game. Card counting, while taking basically the same kind of effort at Spanish 21 as at regular blackjack, does not offer as many opportunities for reward. However, card counting did have some impact on the game.

Fred did several computer simulations using Stanford Wong's excellent software program *Blackjack Count Analyzer.* Here's what he discovered. Using various counting systems, the best edge a card counter could get at Spanish 21 was a *maximum* of 0.5 percent. However, this edge entailed a monumental betting spread of 1 unit in neutral and low counts up to a staggering 30 units during those rare moments when the count favored the player. He discovered that the shoe only became somewhat favorable for betting purposes around 5 percent of the time. To achieve merely a break-even game at Spanish 21, a player needed a betting spread of approximately 1 to 12. Compared to regular six-deck blackjack with good rules, counting at Spanish 21 is essentially a waste of time. Even if you were to tackle it, a betting spread of 1 to 30 would need a huge bankroll to sustain the player as the fluctuations would be immense. In a regular six-deck game, you can expect the shoe to favor you approximately one-fifth of the time. A betting spread of 1 to 6 or 1 to 8 units would be more than sufficient to give an expert card counter around a (slightly more or less) 0.5 percent overall edge. With 6 or 8 units as your maximum bet, the fluctuations would be nowhere near as intense as at Spanish 21.

As disappointing as the above sounds, it is no secret that the casinos are not about to put another game on their floors that players can readily beat. When regular blackjack first made its appearance, no one—not casinos, not players—knew that the game could be beaten. It took many years and many brilliant individuals to discover that the regular casino game of blackjack could be theoretically and *practically* beaten by employing the proper playing strategies and card counting methods. While Spanish 21 can be *theoretically* beaten, it can't be practically beaten without making huge bets in those rare times when the game favors the player—huge bets that could sink a player should he lose them. Keep this in mind: as I stated earlier in this chapter (but it does bear repeating), saying that a shoe favors a player at a given moment of play is not the same as saying that the player is guaranteed a win. On the contrary, the player who ups his bets in positive situations—only to lose—finds himself in quite a hole. In the long run, with a sufficient bankroll to weather bad economic storms, the player will profit because of the positive moments. But the buffeting a player can take getting to that winning long run can be quite intense and highly deflating both to a player's ego and to his bankroll.

In fact, the removal of the 10-spots has stripped the game of the hands that win the most money for the players—20s and blackjacks. In a six-deck game fully 72 percent of the player's positive expectation comes from these two hands alone. The rest come from the hands of 11, 10-9, 10, A-9, and A-8 respectively. The reason that the hard totals of 11 and, to a lesser extent, 10 are so powerful has to do with all the doubling opportunities they present to the regular basic-strategy blackjack player. These doubling opportunities get more money on the table when doing so is to the player's advantage. Unfortunately these favorable doubling opportunities are the very ones diminished in Spanish 21 by the removal of the 10-spots.

If You Insist

However, let's assume that the rather bleak card-counting outlook for Spanish 21 does not faze you. You insist that you still want to count cards at Spanish 21. Assuming that you already know how to count cards at regular blackjack, there are several strategies that you can use to maximize your potential. (If you don't already know how to count cards, I recommend that you read my book *Best Blackjack* or Fred Renzey's book *Blackjack Bluebook*.) First, assume that the shoe starts at a true count of minus 4 (running count of minus 24). It will (usually) gradually work its way up towards neutral as the game progresses because of the predominance of the small cards (in effect your Hi-Lo count has become an unbalanced count now that the 10-spots have been removed). When the count hits "0," you will revert to traditional basic strategy instead of the Armada Play basic strategy for the play of all hands. When the count goes to true count plus 2 or more increase your bet to 30 units and forget about going for any multiple-card bonus hands in cases where you can bust against a dealer's 2, 3, 4, 5, or 6.

The "Unbalanced" Hi-Lo Short-Cut Count

If you wish to forego having to figure the true count, then begin your counting at the start of the shoe at plus 24. As big cards come out, you subtract from 24, as small cards come out, you add to it. When the count reaches 48, you are now in a favorable betting situation where you can increase your bet. When the count reaches 50, you should have your maximum bet out. Then say a prayer.

Basic Strategy for Six Deck Blackjack w/Surrender H17									
Dealer's Upcard									
Your Hand	2	3	4	5	6	7	8	9	10	A
17-21	S	S	S	S	S	S	S	S	S	S
16	S	S	S	S	S	H	H	SR	SR	SR
15	S	S	S	S	S	H	H	H	SR	H
14	S	S	S	S	S	H	H	H	H	H
13	S	S	S	S	S	H	H	H	H	H
12	H	H	S	S	S	H	H	H	H	H
11	D	D	D	D	D	D	D	D	D	D
10	D	D	D	D	D	D	D	D	H	H
9	H	D	D	D	D	H	H	H	H	H
8 or less	H	H	H	H	H	H	H	H	H	H
	2	3	4	5	6	7	8	9	10	A
A:9	S	S	S	S	S	S	S	S	S	S
A:8	S	S	S	S	D	S	S	S	S	S
A:7	S	D	D	D	D	S	S	H	H	H
A:6	H	D	D	D	D	H	H	H	H	H
A:5	H	H	D	D	D	H	H	H	H	H
A:4	H	H	D	D	D	H	H	H	H	H
A:3	H	H	H	D	D	H	H	H	H	H
A:2	H	H	H	D	D	H	H	H	H	H
	2	3	4	5	6	7	8	9	10	A
A:A	SP	SP	SP	SP	SP	SP	SP	SP	SP	SP
10:10	S	S	S	S	S	S	S	S	S	S
9:9	SP	SP	SP	SP	SP	S	SP	SP	S	S
8:8	SP	SP	SP	SP	SP	SP	SP	SP	SR	SP
7:7	SP	SP	SP	SP	SP	SP	H	H	H	H
6:6	SP	SP	SP	SP	SP	H	H	H	H	H
5:5	D	D	D	D	D	D	D	D	H	H
4:4	H	H	H	SP	SP	H	H	H	H	H
3:3	SP	SP	SP	SP	SP	SP	H	H	H	H
2:2	SP	SP	SP	SP	SP	SP	H	H	H	H

H=hit; S=stand; D=doubledown; SP=split; SR=surrender

6

Know Your Enemy!

If King Philip had listened to his closest advisors and tempered his enthusiasm for a great naval armada to tackle the pesky British, instead of saying the equivalent of "I want to! I want to, therefore I will!"—it is quite possible that a different Spanish Armada, built carefully over a much longer period of time, with greater attention to detail, speed design and seaworthiness, manned with captains and sailors who had had their beards shaken in storm and skirmish before they took on Her Majesty's best, might have given a much better account of itself. Unfortunately, the Spanish Armada has become something of a joke of history. In the excellent British sitcom of the 1970s, *Fawlty Towers*, written by and starring John Cleese and Connie Booth, there is a moment when the Spanish waiter, Manuel, has been blamed for a series of "cock-ups" (screw ups) that are actually the result of the owner Basil Fawlty's impulsive nature. In blaming Manuel for the situation that has occurred, Basil states: "God knows how they (the Spanish) ever got an Armada together!" The audience duly laughs at this historical jibe and Basil thinks he's covered his tracks.

In some ways the casinos are taking the players for King Philips and they have floated Spanish 21 out on their green and blue felt seas to see if we'll jump into battle before we are truly prepared. In my observations of various Spanish 21 tables to date, I can tell you that almost no one I saw playing the game was playing anything even approaching the correct strategy. The Armada Play basic strategy is meant to cut the edge to its minimum so that the players have a chance to sink the mighty casinos. Unfortunately, too many players have sailed into their battle against the casinos the way the Spanish Armada sailed into its battle against the British—without a proper battle plan and without adequate weaponry. And a battle plan that includes proper weaponry is absolutely necessary if you are going to wade into the fray at Spanish 21. This battle plan must combine two elements:

1. A full understanding of the opponent you are facing, which includes his weaponry, psychology and tactics.

2. A carefully prescribed counterattack against him.

Despite the fact that Spanish 21 has an edge for the casinos (small though it is), there are better and worse ways of playing the game based on the above two factors.

Our Opponent: The Casino
The "DPH" Factor

Why would the casinos of America introduce a game with such a low house edge? Most of the new table games the casinos introduce have house edges ranging from 2 percent to 5 percent or more. Many of the new slot machines have edges sometimes flirting with the double digits. Why then introduce a game with an edge in the measly cents per $100 wagered as opposed to the meaty dollars per $100 wagered?

Because the truth, the whole truth, and nothing but the truth of Spanish 21 is not completely contained in that seemingly small house edge of .82 percent. In fact, a $5 bettor at Spanish 21 could conceivably lose almost as much real money in the long run as a $5 bettor at roulette—a game that has a whopping 5.26 percent edge for the house. How can that be?

Time.

Time is the Janus-faced friend/foe of the casino gambler. Manipulated properly by the player, time can be on our side in terms of comps, in terms of enjoyment, and in terms of giving ourselves the best possible chance to get lucky. Manipulated by the casinos, time is the great destroyer of our discipline, our bankrolls, and our mental balance.

Here's why:

The key to real money-making for the casinos is not necessarily or only the mathematical edge a given game has but the relationship of that edge to something called decisions per hour (DPH). A game such as roulette might conceivably have as few as 25 decisions per hour at a crowded table while a game such as Spanish 21 could have upwards of 100 decisions per hour at its equivalent. Take that $5 bettor and plug in the house edge with the DPH and let's see what could happen.

The $5 roulette player makes 25 wagers in one hour. That's a total of $125 wagered in that hour. The edge for the casino is a rather large 5.26 percent. The player will therefore theoretically lose $6.58 in that hour. Now, the $5 Spanish 21 player will bet $500 in that same hour if he is playing 100 hands per hour. His loss will be $4.10—a difference of only $2.48 when compared with roulette! However, the difference between Spanish 21 and roulette percentages is a hefty 4.44 percent. Yet, for an hour of *playing time* the real monetary difference between roulette and Spanish 21 could be dramatically less than just the edge would indicate.

I have, of course, purposely set up a very dramatic comparison between a rather slow roulette game and a rather fast Spanish 21 game to make my point. In all negative expectation games, no matter how small the house edge, speed increases that edge's impact and that edge's power in the real world. The casinos know this and the players had better know this or they are courting disaster.

Spanish 21 is a fast game. Granted, it's fun. Granted, it's good. Granted, its mathematical edge is quite reasonable as casino games go. But don't ever take for granted the impact a fast dealer can have on such a fast game. That is the first weapon the casino employs against the Spanish 21 player—speed. Because the game is fun, players will tend to want *more* fun and more fun inevitably means more decisions per hour. Remember this, the key variable between the Spanish Armada and the British warships when all else was said and done was *speed!*

The "PSI" Factor

In modern parlance "psi" has come to stand for psychic abilities of the paranormal kind. Discussions of the possibility of abilities such as telekinesis (mind over matter), telepathy (mind-to-mind-communication), and clairvoyance (distance viewing without being physically present) are bandied about in ESP (extra-sensory-perception) circles as readily as discussions of laundry soap are bandied about in laundromats. Whether such psychic phenomena exist in real life is open to question, but there is no doubt the casinos have a PSI factor all their own—in their case, PSI stands for "psychologically stimulating individuals." Next to the house edge and the DPH, the PSI is the big weapon of the casinos against the players. But it is a stealth weapon that not many players are aware of until it plants a bomb right in their heads.

The goal of the PSI factor is to overstimulate and then manipulate the player's psyche in such a way as to make us want to play longer hours for bigger stakes than we originally intended. This is done in a variety of ways, not the least of which is the substitution of colorful chips for drab money in an attempt to make us think that playing with colorful chips is just that—playing *with chips* and not *real money.* Next, the casinos have generally set up spectacularly colorful, high-energy environments where the collective flow of anticipatory adrenaline from countless players mingles with the jingle-bell rock and roll of those ubiquitous slot machines, occasionally intertinged by the jungle roars of craps Tarzans in the ecstasy of a kill. Add to this all those spinning wheels and flashing lights, all those free drinks served to us by seductively uncovered cocktail waitresses (and lately some cocktail waiters) that will loosen our collective gambling libidos (as well as our libido libidos) and make us sitting ducks for the casino edge and DPH to shoot us down.

What the casinos are doing to unwary players is called *sensory overload*. Sensory overload causes a psychological condition sometimes referred to as shock. What is shock? It is our built-in protection when we are overloaded and in danger of being emotionally swamped. What does shock do for us? Sometimes it relaxes us and sometimes it puts us into a kind of torpor. People who are in shock—perhaps from a major accident or catastrophe—will often act calmly and coolly and seem for all intents and purposes quite rational. It isn't until after the fact (be it the fact of a car accident, the fact of the death of a loved one, or the fact of an earthquake, etc.) that the person crumbles and goes to pieces. Ever look around at the casinos and see people who seem mesmerized? Who seem to be calmly playing and losing tens, hundreds, thousands and tens of thousands of dollars with nary a blink of an eye? How calm, how cool, how relaxed they do seem. In fact, some of these people are involved in severe accidents at the very moment you're observing them—the accident of bad luck!—and they are really in a kind of shock.

It isn't until after they go back to their rooms, or homes, that the full weight of what just happened hits them. "I lost how much money?" an interior voice cries out. That interior voice was the very voice that was stilled during overload, that was swamped by the PSI factor of the casinos.

Sensory overload can work in other ways too. Instead of acting as a soporific and putting us in torpor, it can act as a super stimulant—a speed ball every bit as disorienting as an injection of methamphetamine.

I have a niece whose name is Anna. At this writing she is a lovely six years old. When Anna gets stimulated she runs around the room—literally runs around the room. She can't sit at supper. She can't sit and play. She can't sit still. She runs and runs and runs around the room. At some point she drops and we'll find her contentedly sleeping in some nook or cranny of the house—a blissful little angel who moments before had been a speed demon. In fact, when the beautiful A.P. and I get harried or otherwise wound up, we often say: "I'm Anna running around the room today!" The world of the casino is a world populated by hundreds and thousands of Annas running around the room. They are so stimulated that they don't know they are exhausted. Unfortunately before these casino Annas drop off to dreamland, their money has usually been dropped down the casino drain.

In fact, if you have ever gone to Circus Circus casino in Las Vegas, you will see the "Anna Phenomenon" in full swing—among children *and* adults. Just look around and you'll see hundreds of overloaded kids running, whooping, whining, crying and clambering all over the place. In the casino, you will see many of their parents in the same state. The difference between the two, child and parent, is merely one of perception. Most of us can readily see the overload in children because children are so obvious about it. Adults, especially adults in shock, can often hide it better. They appear to be behaving rationally when instead they are Annas running crazily, albeit metaphorically, around the room.

Make no mistake about this. The casinos exist to take our money. That's not a startling revelation and it doesn't make the casino industry some kind of Great Satan. If you think clearly about this, you realize that movies, plays, bowling, health clubs, restaurants and countless thousands of businesses exist to take our money, too. Most of you reading this book are able to exist because you are taking someone else's money as well. That's capitalism and that is fine with me. Movies, plays, bowling—and *you*—also give something in return for the money being taken: a product, a service, an expertise or an experience. People willingly part with their money if they think what they are getting in return is worth it. They resent it, however, when the return is not equal to the perceived investment. Just think of the last rotten movie you saw that cost eight dollars (or more) and several buckets of expensive "butter-flavored" popcorn. Think of what a waste of money you felt that movie was. Now, think of the great movies you've seen—rarely would you have bemoaned the cost of them because you had too good a time. It is only when the experience, whatever experience that may be, is unpleasant that we kick ourselves (or just kick) and vow not to do it again.

The casinos are much like movies in this way. They give us something for the dollars that we bring. The casinos give us the chance to take home some dollars that we didn't bring—*their* dollars. They also offer us the thrill of competition as we attempt to take their dollars. Casino gambling is athletics without the muscle pulls or the annoyance of having to be in physical condition—although you have to be in gambling condition! I personally love the chance to challenge the casinos. Done properly casino gambling is every bit as satisfactory as the best movie you've ever seen. Done foolishly casino gambling is like rancid "buttered-flavored" popcorn and a movie aimed for brain-dead teens.

The casino's games are similar to a department store's wares. But like a huge department store, the casinos want you to see so many things that you just can't get enough of shopping. Therefore, a kind of shop-til-you drop ethic works on the player. This is dangerous and also unnecessary. In fact, the people who fall for this mania are not enjoying themselves at all, because somewhere deep inside them that little muffled voice that will cry out in a day or so, "You idiot!" is even now attempting to crawl its way into the player's consciousness as he or she throws caution and currency to the winds!

It is absolutely crucial for your long and short-term success to play within yourself. In boxing, a manager will tell a fighter to "dictate the pace" to the opponent. A fighter who can dictate the pace to his opponent usually wins. Of course, there are times when the fighter who has been dictated to for seven, eight, or nine rounds lands one big haymaker and knocks out the other guy. These times are rare, although not nearly as rare as those few-and-far between nights when some poor casino gambler, having been hammered from pillar to post, suddenly hits a run of luck that makes him a bundle, or even rarer still, when some lucky so-and-so puts three one-dollar coins in a machine and lines up the Megabucks symbols. If you are relying on a knockout punch to win the day for you in casino gambling then you are falling into a very carefully laid trap. The casinos are dictating your pace.

Note the casino advertising in Las Vegas, Atlantic City, Tunica and casino points East, West, North and South. They all have one thing in common—they extol the virtues of luck, oftentimes BIG luck, that's just around the corner for you. This is done to put you into a mindset to go for the gusto, go for the gold, go for the jackpot of jackpots. Even in games where there are no big jackpots, such as regular blackjack, the average casino gambler dreams his or her dreams of hitting an epic winning streak that can be ridden to that pot of gold at the end of the rainbow. In my book *Best Blackjack*, I tell the story of the "million-dollar bum" who walked into Treasure Island in Las Vegas with $400 and almost walked out with 1.4 million...almost. He had almost done the impossible at blackjack—worked a $400 stake into a million. For many gamblers, that is a dream they have—finding that pot of gold at the end of the rainbow. In truth, play with the idea that a pot of gold awaits you at the end of the rainbow and you could just as easily fall off the rainbow's end and come crashing to the ground—*splat!*

The COMP Factor

Casinos love to advertise all the free and discounted things they give their "preferred" players. In the world of the casinos, these free-bies are called *comps*, which is short for complimentaries.

Comps can be for free or discounted rooms, free or discounted meals at the buffet, the cafe or the gourmet restaurants, free or discounted shows, and invitations to special events or parties. In order to become a "preferred" player, all that is usually necessary is to get rated. This is usually done by securing a player's card from the casino and handing it in to the floorperson when you cash into a game, or putting it into the slot or video-poker machine that you are about to play. The floorperson (or the computer in the machine) then keeps track of your play. The higher the stakes that you play for, the longer the time that you play for those stakes, and the bigger the casino edges (usually referred to as the PC) of the games that you play, will all go into a formula to determine how much you'll get back from the casino in the form of comps. The comping system of the casinos is used as a reward for players and a stimulus for them to continue to play at the comping properties. (The formula for comping is: DPH x PC x hours played x percent returned = comp value.)

On the surface, there is nothing particularly devious or wrong with casinos wanting to reward loyal players by giving those players a percentage of their action back in the form of comps. However, many players overestimate the true value of the comps that they receive and play for much higher stakes than they would normally play for, or they play for longer periods of time than they would normally stay, just to get a comp not worth the either their time, money or effort. In fact, some players are literally *comp crazy*, thinking that the comps the casinos are giving them are actually "free" and not paid for by their potential losses. I have seen low rollers play an extra hour and lose hundreds of dollars to get a comp for the equivalent of a sandwich! I've seen high rollers bet and lose tens of thousands of dollars and then *brag* about the comped suite the casino gave them and the comped gourmet meal the casino gave them, all of which were worth a fraction of their losses. For some comp-crazy players, comps have become the reason to play—and lose—small or large fortunes. A sandwich is a sandwich—whether it's comped or not. A suite is just a big room. A gourmet meal doesn't taste ten times better because it really cost ten times its worth in losses.

Make no mistake about this—the casinos give nothing away for free. Even promotions that don't require a player to place a single bet are used as lures to bring individuals onto the casino's property. Once there, the casino marketing executives know that it is a rare individual who will not place some bets. The rule of thumb is this—people can't bet if they aren't in the casino to begin with. Comps and other promotions get the bodies into the casinos. As a famous boxing promoter (whose name I have forgotten, unfortunately) once said when told that a given arena had thousands of seats: "I don't really care how many seats you have, I care about how many asses I can put in those seats." Comps are the casinos' way of bringing asses onto their properties. But comps are also a true two-edged sword. In the hands of savvy players, the comping system of the casinos can actually return some value for their play. In the hands of fools, the comps can cut their economic heads off.

The DUMB Factor

Preparatory to writing this book, I called Richard Lowfink the originator of the game. Richard had by that time sold the rights to

Spanish 21 to Masque Publishing and he respectfully declined to be interviewed. However, he did say a curious thing. It seems that with the publication of the proper playing strategy for Spanish 21, some of the casinos who were testing the game became annoyed and wanted to know if *he* had revealed the proper way to play it? He hadn't, of course, but nevertheless the trial casinos were not happy that a new strategy had been developed and was being published for the players to buy.

Why were the casinos in a snit?

Because most players who had rushed into the new game had acted like King Philip with his Armada! The players were so anxious to get into the Spanish 21 fray that they were playing the basic strategy for traditional blackjack, or they were playing variations that they had invented that gave the casinos hefty edges of 2 or 3 percent or more over them. The casinos were pleased with the players' dumb play and happily envisioned it continuing indefinitely. The casinos are not as happy when players get savvy—especially when a player can go from giving the casino, say, a 3 percent edge to giving it a mere .82 percent edge. Despite the fact that even the Armada Play basic strategy can only cut the house edge down as opposed to reversing it into a player's edge (as card counting can with regular blackjack), the casinos still prefer to have as big an edge as possible and therefore prefer stupid players to smart players. To do this, most casinos conspire to keep their players as dumb as possible when it comes to proper playing strategies. For example, many casinos now offer courses where they teach players how to play their various games. You'll see signs announcing such instructions in various pits in various casinos. But rarely do you see a casino offer such a course that actually explains the house edges of the various bets, which bets are good and which bets are abominable. Those casino teachers merely teach us *how* to play the game, as opposed to how *best* to play the game. As of this writing, I have taken eight casino "courses" in blackjack, craps and roulette, and not one did more than explain the rudiments of the game. You really can't blame the casinos, or the casinos' teachers. After all, dumb and dumber contribute to the bottom line profits in a hefty way, while smart and smarter detract from the bottom line. Thus, stupidity is rewarded with comps and smiles, and intelligence is rewarded with suspicion. In newspeak: a good player is a bad player for the casino; a bad player is a good player for the casino.

In casinoese then, I want to make you *BAD!*

7

The Armada Ruse How to Sink the Spanish 21 Armada!

You now know what the casino is trying to do to you when you play any of their games. The DPH (decisions-per-hour), the PC (the casino edge), and the PSI factor (psychologically stimulating players) are all working together with COMPS to strip YOU (you) of your money. While Spanish 21 has a reasonably good house edge, the DPH is on the high side, and the game is quite enjoyable to play. This last statement might seem strange—why should a game that is enjoyable to play be dangerous? Because the more fun you have at a given game, the longer you'll want to play that game, that's why. And a game with as many decisions per hour as Spanish 21 can scuttle your bankroll if you aren't wary.

A carefully structured attack on Spanish 21 must start with the proper playing strategy—this we already have in the Armada Play basic strategy for the play of every possible player hand against every dealer upcard. That reduces the house edge to .82 percent. If you want to attempt to count cards at this game, you might be able to realistically chisel a few tenths of a percent from that as well.

However, to truly try to turn the tables on the casinos at Spanish 21 requires that you *drastically slow down the pace* of the game without the casino raters noticing it, while simultaneously getting the pit personnel to rate you as a "typical" player playing the worst possible strategy. This will (hopefully) allow you to receive comps commensurate with the casino's misperceptions. In short, we want the casino to give us back a hell of a lot more in comps for play that is a heck of a lot less deserving.

And here's how we do it:

Slowing Down the Pace

Speed kills. This is as true in casino gambling as it is true in life. Racing cars, racing hearts, and racing romances have all been known to lead to disaster. Drive within the speed limit, exercise to get that pulse rate down, and take care to whom you give your love, and you'll be healthier and happier and, perhaps, live longer. So too with gambling.

If we estimate that Spanish 21 can get in 80 hands per hour, then the expected long-run loss per hour for the Armada Strategy player playing $10 per hand is $6.56. Since most casinos want a minimum of four hours of play for full comping purposes, a $10 Spanish 21 player will lose on average $26.24 for every four hours that he plays. That translates into approximately a two-and-one-half bet shortfall at the end of four hours of play. However, keep this in mind. When we talk about average losses per hour or per four hours, that does not mean that at the end of an hour or four hours of actual play you will be down that exact amount of money. You could be up or down hundreds, perhaps thousands, of dollars more or less than the average. The long-run averages that I cite are just that—long-run averages. The short run, which is where we all basically play, often resembles the long-run the way a worm resembles a giraffe. Still, the more we play a given game over the years, the more that worm begins to take on the characteristics of the giraffe.

Now let us figure what our play is worth in terms of comps to the casinos.

Although very few casinos will reveal their exact formulas for comping, it is generally a known "secret" that the casinos will return between 30 and 50 percent of a player's expected or theoretical loss in the form of comps. Thus, if you were playing $10 per hand for four hours at your favorite casino, you could expect the casino to give you

back between $7.87 and $13.12 in comps. This is assuming that the
casino accurately judges you as an Armada Play basic strategy player
and assesses you at a .82 percent disadvantage. Basically, at this level
of play you could expect to get the buffet for two or the cafe for one.
You might even be able to get a discounted room midweek at some
properties as well. The highest level of comps are called RFB—which
means that your room, food and beverage are on the house—and
these are usually earned with bets of $50 to $100 or more.

The following chart will give us the expected loss per four hours
of play for various betting levels at 80 hands per hour and the monetary range of comps we can reasonably expect to get for those betting
levels—if the casinos *accurately* rated us. Assimilate these figures and
then we'll see if we can't trick the casinos into giving us more for less!

Average Bet	Expected Loss per 4 Hrs	Comp Range
$5	$13.12	$3.94 to $6.56
$10	$26.24	$7.87 to $13.12
$15	$39.36	$11.81 to $19.68
$25	$65.60	$19.68 to $32.80
$50	$131.20	$39.36 to $65.60
$100	$262.40	$78.72 to $131.20

The next chart shows the "true loss" for the various betting levels
above assuming the casinos are giving back 40 percent of the expected
loss in the form of comps. The "true loss" is the expected loss minus
the monetary value of the comps. I took 40 percent as the reasonable
return in comps since it is the average of the low of 30 percent and the
high of 50 percent. Again we are assuming that the casino has rated us
as Armada Play basic strategy players at a .82 percent disadvantage.

Average Bet	True Loss per 4 Hrs
$5	$7.87
$10	$15.74
$15	$23.62
$25	$39.36
$50	$78.72
$100	$157.44

The trick is how can we now reduce our expected true loss and perhaps even turn it into an expected true win at Spanish 21? Here's how we do it. The technique is called the *Armada Ruse.*

1. We must decrease the decisions per hour by at least 10 percent to 25 percent.

2. We must increase the casino's *perceived edge* over us from .82 percent to at least 2 percent, if not 3 percent! This will give us back much more in the form of comps and lose us much less in the form of actual money.

The Armada Ruse Step-By-Step

1. Once an hour go to the bathroom right after the first 2 hands of the shoe have been dealt. More often than not, the floor-person watches your first bet and waits to see that you place the same amount for your second bet before recording it on your rating card. Once the second bet is recorded, the floor-person will often head for another table to record bets there as well—and that's *your* cue to head for the *farthest* bathroom. Figure that for every ten minutes you are away from the table, you miss 13 hands. Missing those hands, the casino only has 67 DPH (decisions-per-hour) against you—a reduction of approximately 16 percent!

2. Sit out a hand every now and then. If you sit out one of every ten hands, you reduce the DPH by 10 percent. If you are only playing 67 hands per hour because of your bathroom breaks, you now reduce that by approximately seven hands. You have now reduced the casino's overall DPH to 60! That's a reduction of 25 percent! If you feel funny about sitting out a hand every so often, then count to ten before you make your playing decisions. Remember the dealer has to wait for you to make a decision and while the dealer is trained to deal as fast as he can, he also must follow the rule of the game and give

every player the chance to make his or her decision known before moving on to the next player. Better still, count to ten *and* sit out a hand every so often.

3. *Memorize* the Armada Play basic strategy for the playing of your hands at Spanish 21. Then get a basic strategy chart for *traditional* blackjack (you can usually find these in the gift shops of the casinos or copy it from this book) and bring that to the table. Now, on many of the decisions that are the same between Spanish 21 and traditional blackjack, make sure that you refer to the strategy card. Make sure the pit people see that you are referring to the *traditional* chart. ("I bought this in your gift shop, I sure hope it helps!" or "I photostated this from that guy what's-his-name's book, and it had better work!") The pit will figure you are playing the traditional basic strategy which gives the house a hefty 3 percent or more edge over you. This will then be recorded on your score card. Instead of the casino figuring it has a .82 percent edge over you, it will put its edge at 2 to 3 percent! It will then figure your expected loss to be much, much greater than it actually is and you will be comped accordingly. Referring to the traditional basic strategy chart on most of your decisions will also slow down the game.

4. Play at crowded tables in crowded pits so that the floorperson who is rating you has a lot of people to rate and a lot of things to do. The more people and things that are on his/her mind, the less chance one of them will be you. Crowded tables also set up more chances for someone to win and the others to share the Jackpot Bonus. Crowded tables usually mean much fewer hands per hour per player and this in and of itself will reduce the casino's real bite on your money.

5. Use the casinos' psychology against them. This may seem odd that I am suggesting that the players can—in a sense—"psych out" the casinos but in the case of Spanish 21 this is precisely the what we can do. Why? Because Spanish 21 pits are not as

counter crazy as are traditional blackjack pits for obvious reasons and they really aren't thinking in terms of players beating them in the long run. The casinos are fundamentally convinced that the game of Spanish 21 can't be beaten as can regular blackjack and they are therefore much more interested in seeing that the game runs smoothly and that the trivia of the pit (ratings, comps, who's going to whose house for the barbecue this Saturday, etc.) is handled with efficiency than they are in attempting to catch players who can beat them. The pit crews aren't looking for someone who is betting less in order to get more in comps. This is one big psychological advantage that we have over the casino in Spanish 21—no one is looking for the Armada Ruse. We're blindsiding them!

In regular multiple-deck blackjack games, it is almost a rule of thumb that card counters will attempt to sit out hands when the decks are negative. So anyone who takes a bathroom break mid-shoe could be a suspected card counter. Take several breaks in a session, vary your bet even a little, and they'll probably call the eye-in-the-sky to watch your play. In Spanish 21, just about every shoe at every moment is perceived by the pit to be negative (and so it is)—thus a bathroom break is just a bathroom break as opposed to being a way to reduce one's exposure to a low count. It would be rare that the eye-in-the-sky, or the eyes in the heads of the pit crew, will be focused on your play. The Armada Ruse is used to gain the edge by combining comps with a lower disadvantage per hour than the casino believes you have.

6. Make sure that the pit thinks of you as a gambler interested in getting rated. Give your name in and ask to be rated. Be eager and enthusiastic about getting comps. As you will see, utilized properly, the Armada Ruse can turn the monetary expectation of Spanish 21 in your favor.

How the Armada Ruse Turns a Negative into a Positive

Let us see what happens if we can apply the above scenario of the Armada Ruse perfectly. Let us take a person who makes a $25 average bet. In four hours of play, such a player can expect to lose $65.60. The true loss would be $39.36 because of the comps the player can expect to get if the casino judged him at a .82 percent disadvantage. That's the game played the casino's way.

Now, we play it the Armada way.

Instead of betting $25 over 80 decisions, we are only betting $25 over 60 decisions, so our expected loss is really only $49.20 instead of $65.60. The overworked and harried casino rater (who we have called over and anxiously and happily given our player's club card to) perceives us as still playing 80 hands but with a 2 or 3 percent edge in favor of the house—not the true edge of .82 percent. That's because we appear to be playing the traditional basic strategy for the play of the hands. ("Yep, I like the way they color-coded what I'm to do on this card I just bought at the gift shop!" or "I hope that Scobleet, or Scabloot or however you pronounce his name knows what he's doin' with this here strategy from his book *Blest Blackjack*.") If the casino rater writes down that we are playing with a 2 percent disadvantage, the casino will assume that we will lose a theoretical $160 in four hours. If it comps us at 40 percent of our perceived loss—the house will return $64 worth of comps! Our real expected loss is $49.20 and the casino returns $64 to us. Voila! We are now turning the tables on them and we are actually ahead $14.80 at the end of four hours! If the casino rates us as playing with a 3 percent disadvantage we wind up being $46.80 ahead! And that, dear readers, is how we sink the game of Spanish 21.

Obviously, in the real rough and tumble waters of casino play, we can't accurately predict exactly how we'll be rated or whether we can actually reduce the DPH by 25 percent without drawing too much attention to ourselves. As a savvy player, you will have to judge just how far you can really push the casino into giving you more for less. But the Armada Ruse is a solid strategy and worth pursuing. There is no doubt that at most casinos even a $10 player war-rants some comps when they put in the requisite time. You will get some of your money back regardless of how you play. But if you can successfully knock down the DPH and get the casino to think you are a DUMB traditional player, then the pit rater will more than likely record an increased PC on your rating. Then take those COMPS and run! In this way, you might actually be able to get a real monetary edge over a game that seems to be invulnerable to traditional black-jack advantage play.

The following charts show the monetary edges of playing the Armada Ruse with the Armada Play basic strategy for various sce-narios. The assumption behind each chart is that 80 hands are played per hour and that each day you play for four hours, although I have broken the win down as a per hour figure as well. I have shown how much you can make for various betting levels and for PCs (house edges) of two and three percent that the casino will apply to average players.

Chart 1 shows a 25 percent reduction from the normal 80 hands. That means you are playing just 60 hands per hour. The casino rates you as facing a 3 percent house edge and returns 40 percent of your expected loss. The expected loss is what the casino figures you will lose betting the amount shown for four hours with a 3 percent house edge. The real loss is what you will lose in the long run betting the amount shown for four hours at 60 hands per hour at a house edge of .82 percent. The real win is the combination of real loss and comp dol-lars returned in the form of food, room and other freebies. The player has an edge of .78 percent.

Chart 1

Avg. Bet	Expected Loss	Real Loss	Comp $	Real Win	Win Per Hr
$5	$48.00	$9.84	$19.20	$9.36	$2.34
$10	$96.00	$19.69	$38.40	$18.72	$4.68
$15	144.00	$29.52	$57.60	$28.08	$7.02
$20	$192.00	$39.36	$76.80	$37.44	$9.36
$25	$240.00	$49.20	$96.00	$46.80	$11.70
$50	$480.00	$98.40	$192.00	$93.60	$23.40
$100	$960.00	$196.80	$384.00	$187.20	$46.80

Chart 2 shows a 10 percent reduction in play from 80 hands. The casino rates you as facing a 3 percent house edge and returns 40 percent of your expected loss. The player has an edge of .51 percent.

Chart 2

Avg. Bet	Expected Loss	Real Loss	Comp $	Real Win	Win Per Hr
$5	$48.00	$11.80	$19.20	$7.40	$1.85
$10	$96.00	$23.60	$38.40	$14.80	$3.70
$15	$144.00	$35.40	$57.60	$22.20	$5.55
$20	$192.00	$47.20	$76.80	$29.60	$7.40
$25	$240.00	$59.00	$96.00	$37.00	$9.25
$50	$480.00	$118.00	$192.00	$74.00	$18.50
$100	$960.00	$236.00	$384.00	$148.00	$37.00

Chart 3 shows no reduction in play from 80 hands. The casino rates you as facing a three percent house edge and returns 40 percent of your expected loss. The player has an edge of .38 percent.

Chart 3

Avg. Bet	Expected Loss	Real Loss	Comp $	Real Win	Win Per Hr
$5	$48.00	$13.12	$19.20	$6.08	$1.52
$10	$96.00	$26.24	$38.40	$12.16	$3.04
$15	$144.00	$39.36	$57.60	$18.24	$4.56
$20	$192.00	$52.48	$76.80	$24.32	$6.08
$25	$240.00	$65.60	$96.00	$30.40	$7.60
$50	$480.00	$131.20	$192.00	$63.80	$15.20
$100	$960.00	$262.40	$384.00	$121.60	$30.40

Chart 4 shows a 25 percent reduction in play from 80 hands. The casino rates you as facing a *2 percent house edge* and returns 40 percent of your expected loss. The player has an edge of .24 percent.

Chart 4

Avg. Bet	Expected Loss	Real Loss	Comp $	Real Win	Win Per Hr
$5	$32.00	$9.82	$12.80	$2.96	$0.74
$10	$64.00	$19.68	$25.60	$5.92	$1.48
$15	$96.00	$29.52	$38.40	$8.88	$2.22
$20	$128.00	$39.36	$51.20	$11.84	$2.96
$25	$160.00	$49.20	$64.00	$14.80	$3.70
$50	$320.00	$98.40	$128.00	$29.60	$7.40
$100	$640.00	$196.80	$256.00	$59.20	$14.80

Chart 5 shows a 10 percent reduction in play from 80 hands. The casino rates you as facing a *2 percent house edge* and returns 40 percent of your expected loss. The player has an edge of .07 percent.

Chart 5

Avg. Bet	Expected Loss	Real Loss	Comp $	Real Win	Win Per Hr
$5	$32.00	$11.80	$12.80	$1.00	$0.25
$10	$64.00	$23.60	$25.60	$2.00	$0.50
$15	$96.00	$35.40	$38.40	$3.00	$0.75
$20	$128.00	$47.20	$51.20	$4.00	$1.00
$25	$160.00	$59.00	$64.00	$5.00	$1.25
$50	$320.00	$118.00	$128.00	$10.00	$2.50
$100	$640.00	$236.00	$256.00	$20.00	$5.00

Chart 6 shows no reduction in play from 80 hands. The casino rates you as facing a *2 percent house edge* and returns 40 percent of your expected loss. The *house* has an edge of .005 percent. Note that under "real win" you actually have a real loss and under "win per hour" you actually have a slight loss per hour.

Chart 6

Avg. Bet	Expected Loss	Real Loss	Comp $	Real Win	Win Per Hr
$5	$32.00	$13.12	$12.80	-$0.32	-$0.08
$10	$64.00	$26.24	$25.60	-$0.64	-$0.16
$15	$96.00	$39.36	$38.40	-$0.96	-$0.24
$20	$128.00	$52.48	$51.20	-$1.28	-$0.32
$25	$160.00	$65.60	$64.00	-$1.60	-$0.40
$50	$320.00	$131.20	$128.00	-$3.20	-$0.80
$100	$640.00	$262.40	$256.00	-$6.40	-$1.60

The above charts are to be used as a reference, but cannot be looked at as unequivocal mathematical statements of house edges since some of the comping game is not strictly formulaic and comping practices change from casino to casino and pit person to pit person within a given casino. So be friendly and fun-loving when you ask the pit for your comps, and you might actually get even more than the comp values stated above—thereby making more money and thereby having a greater edge. In fact, at the $25, $50 and $100 levels, there is a very good chance that your comps will be much higher than I make them out to be—especially if the casino is picking up the cost of your room. Another thing to keep in mind is the fact that while you are indeed beating the casinos at their own games if the Armada Strategies can be implemented fully, you will still not go home—in the long run—with more *real* money than you arrived with. The comps, while they do have a cash value, are not the same thing as cash—you can't take home the monetary value of your hotel room, your comped meals, etc. However, if you were going to play in casinos anyway, if you were willing to pay top dollar for a room, a show, a meal—then you are indeed way ahead of the game when you employ the Armada Strategies. You are, in fact, a winner.

Here is another thing to consider. If you were to add card counting to the Spanish 21 mix, you would be able to increase the edge you have at the Armada Ruse. Now, I am not saying that I would recommend making those staggering 1 to 30 betting spreads to get the edge. On the contrary, a betting spread of 1 to 6 would be enough to add a few tenths of a percent to the Armada Ruse expectations that are cited above without having to worry about enormous fluctuations in bankroll or enormous scrutiny from the pits. It is a thought to consider for those of you who want to wring every last penny that you can from this new and exciting game.

Questions on the Armada Ruse

Wouldn't it be better to use something like the Armada Ruse in regular blackjack where the house only has a 0.5 percent edge?

Yes. The only problem is that the casinos watch regular blackjack for just that type of thing. Most card counters now employ some type of "act" in order to sit out "bad shoes" (definition: low counts) and savvy pit people are aware of this. Once a floorperson suspects that you are counting, he or she will watch your betting spreads. In a multiple-deck game, most players want to get as big a minimum to maximum bet spread as they can. If a floorperson notices a player spreading and *also* sitting out an inordinate number of hands on select occasions, the player might be pegged as a counter and asked to leave or the dealer will be told to cut half the cards out of play. At

Spanish 21, you can sit out every tenth hand and no one will care. You can go to the bathroom and no one will suspect that it is a part of your design to beat them at their own game. While the pits will watch the game, they won't be watching you that closely except to record your bets for comping purposes. In regular blackjack they watch players for comping purposes and for *nailing* purposes.

While it sounds good to use comps as a way to get more from the casinos, I don't like to ask for them. I feel funny about it.

I used to feel that way as well...and I sometimes still do. Most of us have been brought up with the idea (the correct idea in my opinion) that you must earn what you get in this life. But I've had to overcome my feelings about asking for comps and I've done it by making myself believe that I am *entitled* to whatever I can take from the casinos that they are *willing* to give. My good friend, K.F., has gone a long way in helping me in that department. He is a comp wizard and when I play with him, he always asks for something. His motto is: "Food tastes better when it is free." Now, when K.F. plays blackjack he has a 1.0 to 1.5 percent advantage over the casino so in the long run any comps he does get are indeed *free*. Another motto of his is: "If you don't ask, you don't get." And how does he feel about taking a little more than his play might warrant as I suggest you do in the Armada Ruse? "I've worked for my comps by playing and I've worked hard for them by conning. Remember this: the casino does not have to say yes. No one is compelling the casino to give you a comp. They give them for a reason. I take them for a reason. Our reasons are different that's all."

I do understand the hesitancy that you have. Part of it is the fact that if you are turned down for a comp, you might feel like a fool, or a loser. But here's the rub: if comps can mean the difference between being a winning player and being a losing player (and in Spanish 21 they can) then is it more foolish to never ask for a comp (thereby assuring that you will really be a long-term loser) or to ask for a comp and occasionally be turned down and feel temporarily like a loser? I'd rather occasionally feel like a loser and be a winner than know that I am in fact a real loser.

Here's still another way to look at it. Let us say that you have played enough to get a cafe meal—a meal worth, say, $20. However, instead of the food, the casino is now giving you a crisp $20 bill—you just have to ask for it. "Sir, may I have that $20 bill?" Now, sometimes you ask and they say: "No." Sometimes you ask and they say: "Yes." Think of it as free money—a free $20 bill—that more often than not they will place right in your hands. Thought of that way, it isn't all that hard to ask for a comp. "Brother, can you spare a dime!"

I'm thinking of turning pro. Should I play Spanish 21 as well as regular blackjack? I'm sick of my regular job and I think it would be better to be a professional gambler.

I'm assuming the person who wrote this letter to me is an unmarried man, and relatively young, because 99 percent of the people who have asked me the above question, or something similar, have been just that—young guys looking to get out of humdrum jobs. It seems romantic to say "I'm a professional gambler" as it conjures up images of the good life with the casinos funding it. Days by the pool, grapes being carefully put in your mouth by scantily dressed sirens who coo to you about your manliness and love-making prowess. You're Maverick and dangerous Doc Holiday and all those Damon Runyon characters dancing across a Broadway stage. That's the male version of the fantasy anyway. I don't know if there is a female version of the professional gambler's fantasy. The real version is a little less joyful, a little less washed with the sweet scent of female pheromones, a little less informed by testosterone and a lot more involved with drudgery, anxiety and, at times, anguish. There are no grapes by the poolside, and there are no scantily clad sirens waiting for you to finish your grueling casino sessions so that they may please you in any way you desire. In fact, most "pros" are often in no mood to show either their manliness or their love-making prowess after they have played for ten hours in a smoke filled casino. Most professional gamblers I know—even those who can be described as successful— are a miserable lot. Most don't make what I consider to be a good living (say a $100,000 or more a year) and most don't make what I consider to be a living (say $30,000 a year). Most have to scrape by.

The best professional card counter I ever played with lived in a trailer and had to scrounge for a living. Yes, there are a few who can play games such as poker and make millions—they also lose millions. A handful of sports bettors are making a good living—but they are the Michael Jordans of gambling. My advice is to forget turning pro and instead work up a nice big bankroll that will allow you to play regular blackjack as a competent card counter and play Spanish 21 using the Armada Strategies. A steady job is one of the greatest things in this world—you get your paycheck and you know how much it will be. A little husbandry over a few years is enough to give anyone a sufficient bankroll to make trips to casinos a frequent thing. Then you can pretend that you are a professional gambler (as long as you don't try to fool yourself). Those of you reading this who share the sentiments of the young guy who wrote the above, my son Michael has the way to look at it. He once said: "Of course, Dad, people hate to work, that's why they call it *work!* Otherwise they'd call it *fun.*"

The above response is for young people. However, if you are retired and have a decent amount of money coming in—you could become a semipro. That's right. As long as you play within your means, you can use the casino as a source of (a little) extra income, (a lot of) extra excitement, and (plenty of) extra drama. If lying on the beach in Florida prepping your skin to become a pocketbook or wallet is not your thing, then learn to count cards at regular blackjack, and learn to play the Armada Strategies at Spanish 21 perfectly, and you'll find every day a challenge as you go up against the mighty casinos.

Isn't it immoral to make the casinos think you are actually playing more than you really are in order to get them to give you more in comps? What about the idea of having that traditional basic strategy card to make them think you aren't playing the best strategy? Don't you find that all very fishy?

No. Maybe. Yes. It depends on how you look at it. You are not hiding the fact that you are getting up or sitting out hands (even if you sit out hands when the pit person isn't looking). If the casino raters want, they can keep accurate records of how much you are playing. As far as using the traditional basic strategy card to fool them into thinking you're the fool—it's your call. Again any astute pit person can watch you play and, having read this book, know you are using the proper the Armada Play basic strategy for hitting, standing, splitting and doubling. Yes, it is subterfuge in a sense. But remember what I said about Richard Lowfink's statement concerning how angry the trial casinos were when they found out that some people—a handful if that many—might learn how to play a good strategy against Spanish 21. If the casinos are counting on your stupidity to take money from you, then why can't you hope that the casinos will be equally as stupid and overrate what you *don't* know? If you think of what you are attempting to do to the casinos as a battle plan in a war against your enemy—yes, it is civilized, friendly, and enjoyable but it is a war nevertheless—then psychological warfare (the Armada Ruse) is a proper component in the players' arsenal, in addition to the big gun of the Armada Play basic strategy. The casinos do it to the players—they set up the conditions for us to want to win truckloads of money, they give us free drinks to loosen our psychological and physical purse strings, and they rarely give the player the proper strategies to play in their in-house courses. So why shouldn't we do a little psyching of our own? If all that doesn't sway you to think of the full Armada Strategies as proper then don't do it. Use the Armada Play basic strategy for your hands and go to the bathroom when the dealer is shuffling so that you can get in as many hands as the casino wants you to play. As for me—within reason and the law—all's fair in love and casino war!

Are there any good books that go into detail about tricking the casinos?

Yes, there are three books that I recommend reading for really getting yourself into the mind-frame for doing unto the casinos as they do unto us. The first is Max Rubin's *Comp City* and the second is *The Frugal Gambler* by Jean Scott (both published by Huntington Press). The authors of these volumes have put into practice their own versions of the Armada Ruse against various games—Rubin on the high-roller end playing blackjack for relatively large stakes and Scott on the low-roller end playing 25-cent and dollar video poker. I think

Max Rubin was the first writer to coin the phrase "comp wizard" and Jean Scott is known as the "Queen of the Comps." The third book is my own *Guerrilla Gambling: How to Beat the Casinos at Their Own Games!* (Bonus Books), which has extensive sections on how to psych out the casinos and how to psych up yourself for true warfare. While some gambling writers might dismiss the idea that psychology plays a role in table games that are banked by the casino, nothing could be further from the truth. A gambler's mindset is every bit as important as his strategic choices as the above three books explain.

8

The Armada
Money Management
System

Any good money management scheme is usually composed of three parts:

1. An appropriate overall gambling bankroll for the game or games you wish to play.
2. A realistic session stake amount that you are willing—though not anxious —to lose.
3. A plan for when to quit when ahead or behind.

Proper money management cannot turn a bad game into a good game or increase or decrease the odds of winning or losing a given bet or series of bets. However, proper money management can go a long way to increasing your pleasure while you play the games of your choice and to decreasing the emotional havoc that a bad run can generate on your nerves. How you handle your money in real life can often determine what kind of economic future you can expect and how you handle your money in a casino can also do the same thing for the future of your gambling activities. People who enjoy frequent casino experiences must have a tight rein on their bankrolls and their emotions if they want to continue in this fashion. Money management is their key to participating in the casino kingdom.

The Armada Money Management System is strictly geared to Spanish 21 and not to any other game. It takes into consideration that Spanish 21 is your game of choice and that you will be putting into effect the Armada Ruse and the Armada Play basic strategy. You will note that while the return on the Armada Strategies can be considered "positive" because the comp value is overcoming the slight house edge, you will still gradually lose "cash" the longer you play, even though you accrue the attendant comps. Therefore, all the money management advice must be tempered with the idea that you will indeed need to put regular deposits into your gambling account to keep it at the proper levels for the bets you wish to make.

Getting Your Bankroll and Life in Order

I have been on both ends of the bankroll experience. At times, I have played casino games without a bankroll specifically set aside to do so and therefore, I have used money that could be considered money that would be used for other things—"real-life money" so to speak. However, in recent years I have had a nice amount set aside that I use strictly for gambling purposes. Here's the difference between the two extremes as I experienced them.

When I was playing with money that was also used for other things, any loss was a terrible loss and I felt *guilty* about it—even though I had plenty of money and wasn't playing for stakes that could really make a dent in my life, win, lose or draw. Yet, despite this fact and the fact that in the long run I was playing with a slight edge over the casinos, nothing was much of a comfort when I would lose a given session on a given day, or a given day in a given week, or (horrors!) a given week in a given month. Luckily I have (as of this writing at least) never experienced a losing streak that lasted a whole month, although I have had friends and acquaintances endure such a state of affairs. It is not a pretty sight. How do you feel when you play with real money as I have done? Awful when you lose and only *relieved* when you win.

The flip side is much better. Now that I have safely tucked away money in an account that is strictly for gambling purposes, I feel a little sad when I lose and great when I win. I can't say that losing ever is taken lightly (I'm not a good loser), but at least I don't curl up into the fetal position quite as readily on a bad day as I used to when I was playing with what I call "real-life money" as opposed to "playing money." Of the two extremes, having a bankroll that is just for gambling is the way to go. It eases the hard psychological times and makes the good times a heck of a lot better. There are various ways to build a gambling bankroll.

Them's That Has Gets—a Bankroll That Is!

If you have plenty of money already in various savings accounts or investments, just take some of it and put it aside and say: "I dub thee gambling money!" Or take one account and dub it that. Then play with the money from that account based on the charts in this chapter. Over time, you will want to replenish some of the stake as Spanish 21 will whittle away at your cash reserves. You can do this by earmarking a given percentage of your yearly interest for the gambling bankroll. Do your own version of Scarlet O'Hara: "As God is my judge, I vow to the heavens to take 10 percent (or 25 percent or whatever) of all my interest earned in a year and put it in my gambling account! And I will never gamble with scared money ever again!" Any wins go into the gaming bankroll as well until you hit whatever you consider to be the magic figure that allows you to take money out of the gambling bankroll and use it for real life.

Thrifty and Nifty Bankroll Creation

If you don't have a number of accounts with money just itching to be set aside for gambling, if you are not in any position to dub anything a gambling bankroll, *but* you still long to play without the guilt attached to losing real-life money, then you are going to have to accrue a gambling bankroll over time. You can do this in a number of ways.

Open an account that is strictly for gambling and put, say, $25 into it for starters. Then, take 1 to 5 percent of your weekly take-home pay and put it in the account until you get enough money to go out and attack the game of Spanish 21. How much of a gambling bankroll would that be? That depends on two factors—how much of an emotional rollercoaster you're willing to ride and how much the stakes are that you want to play for. The best advice I can give would-be Armada Strategists is to get the bankroll first and then pursue your dream of conquering Lady Luck on the high casino seas.

If your take-home pay is $500 per week, then set aside $25 per week. In only twenty weeks, you will have $500 in the bank that will be used strictly and solely for gambling. In a year, you will have $1,300. Check the charts and see where $500 and/or $1,300 will place you on the betting map. Keep this in mind—don't stop putting that $25 per week in the account even after you accumulate what you consider to be a sufficient bankroll to venture into a casino. Remember that you will have to—at some time—replenish your stake so you might as well do it continuously and painlessly. Likewise, any wins that you have go to the stake until you have enough money to play at the level you desire. If you want to go over and above that $25 a week (or whatever figure you're toying with in your head), then consider these questions:

1. Are you playing a lottery such as Lotto or Powerball on a weekly or biweekly basis? If you are, stop playing these useless games and put the money you would have spent on them into your gambling account. An extra $5 per week is an extra $260 a year in your gambling account.

2. Are you one who buys on impulse, often the type of things that wind up in the attic or basement? On the next impulse to buy some worthless thing say: "I don't need that figurine of King Philip, after all, where would I put it? Instead, I'll take the $85.37 that I would have spent on that worthless statue and put it into my gambling account." However, don't say: "Does Tiny Tim really need that operation? I'll just take the $5,000 that would have saved his life and put it in my gambling

bankroll." A little discernment is necessary to distinguish frivolous expenses from important ones.

3. Next, head for the basement or the attic and look around with this thought: "What can I sell?" When you answer the question—then sell it! Have a garage sale, a yard sale, a telephone-your-friends sale. Call some of your pack-rat relatives and give them bargains. "Aunt Daisy, I have this great figurine of King Philip, the one who launched the Armada, yeah, I'll sell it to you for five bucks." Get some money for all the junk that you have accumulated and put whatever you make into your gambling account. You'll be surprised how much you can save in a little time. The younger you are the easier it will be to accumulate huge bankrolls over time if you set your mind to it. (But keep this in mind—you can lose those huge bankrolls if you play the wrong games or the right games the wrong ways.) However, don't say the following: "Yes, local real estate agent, I have this great house that I want to sell so I can acquire a gambling stake and, just to make the deal a little sweeter, I'll throw my Aunt Daisy in—at no charge—on the side along with a figurine of King Philip!"

You should pursue the creation of a serious gambling bankroll in a serious way. You've invested some money in learning the game by buying this book, now invest the proper amount of time to get the proper amount of money to play the game properly. Players who play on short stakes are usually short-tempered and short sighted. Take your time and build that stake up.

The Session Stake

The total amount of money that you put aside for gambling purposes is called your bankroll or your stake. However, you do not go into a casino on a given day with that entire stake—that's way too risky. Instead, you break that bankroll into separate session stakes so that you never have to worry that one session might be so devastatingly awful that it could wipe you out. How many session stakes you divide your bankroll into is largely up to you. As a conservative player, I like to know that I have at least ten session stakes to play with during any given three-day trip to the casinos. Therefore, I take 10 percent of my entire bankroll and that is considered my session stake.

You can approach the question of how much of a bankroll you need to play ten sessions in one of two ways. You can say something like this: "I have saved up $2,000 and therefore I will have $200 per session as my stake. How much should I play for as an average bet?" Or you can say something like this: "I want to play at $25 a hand. How much of a total bankroll will I need to do that?"

Again, I am going to state what I do. You might be more aggressive (less chicken) or you might be more conservative (more chicken) than I am. You'll have to fit what I'm recommending into your scheme of things. The more aggressive you are, the more likely you are to win big and lose big.

The formula I use for Spanish 21 is the forty unit rule of thumb. I want at least forty times my average bet as my session stake. Then I want ten times that amount as my bankroll—translated that would be 400 units. Thus, a $10 player would want to have $400 for a single session of play and $4,000 in the bank. A session stake of forty units is enough to weather even the worst losing streaks and still give you some cushion to make a comeback. The most hands I ever lost in a row was fourteen, although I do know someone who lost twenty. I also heard of someone who won twenty-three hands in a row at the Maxim in Las Vegas, and there are stories of individuals who have won nine out of ten hands for days on end (these are the stories that have become legendary in gaming circles around the country). Still, you can expect frequent streaks of four or five losses in a row, interrupted by occasional winning streaks of the same length. With a forty unit session stake, it would be rare to lose it all in one awfully bad run. Forty units can give you plenty of playing time at Spanish 21.

How many sessions a day should a player play? Three sessions per day would not be an unusual number to plan. You could play one session in the morning, one in the afternoon, and one after dinner. I would not recommend playing more than four hours on any given day in the same casino since there are only so many comps a casino can give you. You can only stay in one comped room and eat one comped dinner at a time. If you intend to play for more than four hours on a given day, then consider giving another casino your action as well. Then you will have built up comp points at two places for the same overall risk. If four hours essentially gets you all the complimentaries you can expect at one casino, it is self-defeating to give that same casino even more hours with no return. That lessens your edge. Go to another casino.

There is one caveat to the above. Some casinos will reward players who play for moderate stakes but play for long periods of time. You might love to play and have a bankroll that allows you to bet $30 per hand for four hours or $15 per hand for eight hours. If you know that you want to play the eight hours, then reduce your average bet to $15. If the casino gives extra for the extra time, you will get the equivalent comps for $15/8 hours as you would have for $30/4 hours. Although all my calculations are based on four hours, you have to analyze yourself to decide where you fit into the time frame. You might want to play more than four hours, you might want to play less. You could increase or decrease your average wager accordingly and probably still get the same value back in comps. How do you know how a casino will judge you? Ask! "Mr. Pit Person, if I play $30 for four hours what will I get in the way of comps? If I play $15 for eight hours will I get the same thing?" Most casino pit people will answer your questions forthrightly. Those that don't? Take your action elsewhere.

I Want to Play a Lot!

The idea of breaking up your bankroll into ten session stakes composed of forty units each assumes that you will go to a casino at least three times and play three sessions per day. You have nine session stakes with one in reserve (an economic and psychological cushion). I realize that three times could be one visit of three days or it could be three trips of one day. But more and more people want to go to casinos as often as they can get away. Casino gambling has

become so popular that more people go to casinos than go to all professional athletic contests combined. More people go to casinos
than go to the movies! If you are interested in going more than three
days a year, then for each additional day you intend to visit add
another session stake. Thus, for the $10 bettor, three days would
require a total bankroll of $4,000 but four days would require a
bankroll of $4,400, while five days would require a bankroll of
$4,800 and so forth. Because forty units is such a conservative ses-
sion stake amount, you don't have to increase your total stake proportionally as you make more and more trips. In fact, many gaming
writers would think that forty units is way too conservative and
would recommend a session stake half that size. Again you be the
judge of your own personality. I love the comfort of knowing that
the casino will never wipe me off the map short of me having a losing streak of herculean proportions. I like that forty unit session
stake for that reason. More than likely you will not get close to losing even a single session stake during the bad times and just as
likely you'll be adding a little here and a little there to your stake as
you have winning sessions. Still, you will, at some time or other as
I have indicated, need to replenish some of your gambling stake as
the house edge whittles away at it. As stated this can be done gradually by depositing a set amount in your gambling account weekly
or monthly.

Here is another thing to consider. You might start off with $4,000
as a total bankroll, win some money, add some money from your
weekly allotment and find that soon you are at the $8,000 mark. You
could continue to play $10 a hand with a nice fat economic cushion
under you or you could, if you wanted, go to $20 a hand. It's your
call.

The following chart will show you how much money you need
in your bankroll to play a given average bet based on forty units per
session, with a ten session bankroll. The assumption is that you plan
to play four hours a day. If you plan to play, say, two hours a day, you
can cut everything in half.

Size of Bankroll	Session Stake	Average Bet
$400	$40	$1
$800	$80	$2
$1,200	$120	$3
$1,600	$160	$4
$2,000	$200	$5
$4,000	$400	$10
$6,000	$600	$15
$10,000	$1,000	$25
$20,000	$2,000	$50
$30,000	$3,000	$75
$40,000	$4,000	$100

When To Quit a Session

A session stake must be thought of as sacred. You must not profane it by adding any more money to it if things are going badly. Doing so might end up in a major loss of much of your bankroll. If you have a rotten night and lose all forty units, obviously that session is over. Don't chase your losses. You wait until the next session to start again. And don't try to con yourself either by saying something like this: "Well, I just lost my forty unit session stake, that session is over. Now, I'll start my second session!" No. Wait at least a couple of hours before you begin a new session. Take a walk. Take a nap. Take a break.

I realize that theoretically it doesn't matter when you begin or end sessions as the math of blackjack looks at all play as just one long continuous session. But math is not a man or woman. Math can't get depressed. Math doesn't increase its bets in the hope it will get back everything in one orgy of winning. Math is not conscious of how awful it feels to lose. Math doesn't need to take a nap or a nice long walk to clear its head of negative or destructive thoughts. Math is just numbers and, while numbers never lie, they don't always tell the absolute truth of the human condition.

One of the best professional card counters I ever played with was the late Paul Keen. At one particular time he was having a horrible two week run where it seemed he couldn't win anything. Finally he said: "I'm taking a week off." I asked him why. He laughed and said: "Because I want all the cards all over the world to get thoroughly shuffled before I play again." What did he really mean? "I need a rest because I've been taking a pounding." A session where you lose your entire session stake is a small pounding. Take a couple of hours off and let all the cards all over the world get shuffled a few extra times before you play again.

Short of losing your entire stake, there are other ways to determine when to call a session quits at Spanish 21. If you have planned on playing, say, three sessions in a given day, you could, as a rule of thumb, figure that no one session will last more than an hour and a half—that is if you are losing (I'll discuss winning a little later on). So let us say that you are at the one-and-a-half-hour mark and you're down five or ten or however many units. Push your chips to the dealer and say: "Color me up." You're done for that session. You hadn't gone anywhere, you gave it your best shot, now take a break. What do you do with the extra units that you didn't lose, the remaining units of your session stake? You take that money *home* with you. It goes back into the bankroll. You don't add it to the next session stake for that trip. A session stake is sacred money—you win with it, you lose with it—but whatever is left over, win, lose or draw, goes home with you, period.

What happens if you are even at the end of an hour and a half? You could quit. You could play one more hand. If you lose that hand you quit. If you win—then play another hand for half the amount of your average bet so that if you lose that you will end the session ahead anyway. If you win that half-bet, then bet a whole bet on the next hand. Play until you lose a hand...then quit. If you find that a positive run has occurred and you want to play a few more hands, then give yourself a two or three bet loss limit before you call it a session. Once you are at the end of a session, you don't want to go from the black into the red at the last moment.

There are some sessions that you might want to abruptly cut short. For example, you lose ten hands in a row and find that sweat is pouring out of every pore of your poor body. Your shirt is drenched. People are looking at you with funny expressions on their faces. You find that you feel awfully light-headed and want to sink into your seat. The dealer might jokingly say something like: "I've been doing that all day. Five guys have killed themselves because of me today, ha! ha!" You might think to yourself: "Maybe I should take a short walk and then come back?" If you think that, then do that. The math says it doesn't matter whether you've lost one, two, ten, twenty or one-hundred hands in a row but your mind says that it does. Listen to your mind. Take a breather...then get back into the trenches.

Stopping when you're ahead is a bit more complicated as you *never quit while you're winning.* Here again the human experience is slightly at odds with the mathematical model. Math tells us that you can never judge what you're in, only what you *were* in. You also can't tell what will happen, only the probabilities of what might happen. Fine. Here's the scenario: You have won quite a bit of money, say fifty units, and now you think to yourself: "Should I leave?" The answer is: "Not yet." First see if your streak will continue. Place a bet and say: "If I win this I'll keep playing until I lose two hands in a row." If you keep winning, keep playing. If you lose two hands in a row, then quit. That's what I mean when I say *never quit while you're winning.*

The other way to approach this fifty unit win is to say: "I'll take twenty-five units of my fifty unit win and put it aside, along with my forty unit session stake. This money is now locked up in my bank—that's sixty-five units. I'll play with the twenty-five units until I win another fifteen units or lose the twenty-five units." If you win the fifteen units you can quit or say: "I'll now take the fifteen units and only play with that. I'll take the twenty-five units I was playing with and add it to my bank. I now have ninety units in my bank. I'll play until I lose the fifteen units or win fifteen units." If fortune shines on you and you keep winning, keep taking a certain amount of the win and put it away and play with a small portion of the remainder. If this lasts until you fall asleep at the table, so be it. When you're carried semicomatose to your room is when such a winning session will end. Again, *never quit while you're winning.*

Tongue out of cheek, you get the idea. If you keep testing the waters, and you keep winning, then keep playing. However, the reverse could happen. Say you have that fifty unit win. Now, you take twenty-five units and play with that and lose it all. The session is over. You take your forty unit stake and your twenty-five unit win and you take a break. The next session you start with your next session stake.

It is in the great in-between—in that gray nether world between an obvious loss and an obvious win—where when to end a session calls for a little intuition as opposed to a lot of advice from me. In the great in-between—you've won three, six, ten, thirteen, eighteen units or so—is where you have to analyze (or intuitively recognize) several factors and then make a decision:

1. The time you've already played.
2. The win you've already achieved.
3. The fatigue you may already be experiencing.
4. The comps you've already garnered.

In experienced players, a "little voice" in their heads often tells them it's time to go. You can almost feel the moment: "Scobe, the session is over." However, the "little voice" never says something like this: "Bet the ranch, Ray baby, I feel lucky!" or "Helga, to hell with Mama Grendal's knee surgery. Bet it up!" If you hear a "little voice" in your head saying something like the aforementioned, you have been possessed by the gambling demon and need a good exorcism...or a bad lounge act. For those who don't have that "little voice" I have prepared a list of questions for you to answer. If any answer to any question is yes, then you can call it a session.

1. Are you becoming tired?
2. Have you made a mistake or several mistakes in the Armada Play basic strategy?
3. Are you becoming hesitant to double down or split because you are afraid to lose the small win that you have?
4. Are you beginning to think of taking a nap or a walk?
5. Have you already asked for and received a comp?
6. Is there something else you have begun to think about such as going shopping, going to a show, taking a shower, reading one of Frank Scoblete's books?

7. Have you played a sufficient amount of time to satisfy your need for action?
8. Are you beginning to feel that this session is one where you should be satisfied with that small win?
9. Are people at the table beginning to annoy you?
10. Are you beginning to feel neck strain, eye strain, or back strain?

Some gamblers can't stand the thought of putting in time and only coming out with a small win. Some gamblers have bought into the casino's carefully crafted concept that the only good win is a big win. Well, to me every win is a good win because a win—any win—is by definition good. Of course, we'd all like to have those magic moments when Lady Luck becomes our love slave and gives us our heart's desire—a huge, huger, and even huger-than-that win. But at the end of some time at the table, as the "little voice"—or the "yes" answers to one of the questions above—tells us to leave with the little win, then we should leave, pronto, posthaste, right now. The beautiful A.P., my wife and playing partner, always says: "A win's a win!" She also says: "Savor the win!" To that I say: "Amen, sister!"

A Cautionary True Tale

In the Spring 1998 issue of my magazine *The New Chance and Circumstance* [published by Paone Press, Box 610, Lynbrook, NY 11563], appeared one of the best accounts of what NOT to do as a player. It was written by Edward Wile and it graphically and honestly explained how an individual can go on "tilt." Going on tilt means losing one's cool along with one's money in a casino. Wile's is one of the best descriptions I have ever read of the phenomenon—one just about every casino gambler experiences at one time or another. I think it appropriate that it appears at the end of this chapter as it is much easier on the nerves to learn from another's misfortune than it is to actually experience that misfortune yourself. Although Mr. Wile is recounting his experiences at regular blackjack, the lesson is applicable to any and all casino games, including Spanish 21.

I went down to Atlantic City during the day on Wednesday. I am a perfect basic strategy player who has read the books, and can count, but I don't, because I do not have, and never will have, an adequate bankroll. Thus, I consider myself a recreational once-a-month player, who bets essentially in a progression, hoping to get lucky.

In a year of play the best I've done is break even, but mostly I lose part of the money I brought with me. But typically I have a nice meal, a few laughs with buddies, so it's OK...good entertainment.

This Wednesday, since I was on vacation, I decided to head down by myself. I took the bus from Port Authority. I brought 200 dollars. Got down to AC at 2:30 PM. Cashed in my coupon for $16.50 at The Claridge, and walked over to Bally's because I had a coupon that they sent me for $5.00 cash. So I cashed my coupon, and headed out to the Wild, Wild, West casino to look for a five-dollar table, which I did indeed find!

I bought in for 60 bucks and off we go. Forty-five, possibly 50, minutes of play and I'm up 50 dollars. Of course, being...greedy...the casino bumps the table limit up to 10 dollars. I lose a couple of hands and I take off.

It's a little after four and I'm starving, feeling good about my success. So it's off to my favorite lunch spot, Billy's Diner/Liquor Store on the boardwalk. Great diner food at reasonable prices served by friendly folks. A tasty turkey burger and a large Coke and I'm out on the boardwalk.

I love this place!

Where to? Sands five-dollar pit or Resorts? I decide on Resorts. I like the back poker room a lot. But when I get there it's closed. Damn.

I head out to the main casino. One circle around the floor and I see no five dollar tables. I ask a pit boss if there are any five-dollar games and he sends me to the opposite end of the room. There are no five-dollar tables there. I ask another pit boss and he sends me back to the other side.

"I already looked there. Is it possible that there are no five-dollar tables?" I asked.

"That is possible," he responds.

There clearly are no five-dollar tables. I know that with my $240 I should NOT play at a $10 table, but I really don't feel like walking back to the Sands, and I'd probably have to wait a while to get a seat, so I do exactly *what the casino* expects *me to do. I decide to stay and play at a $10 table. Perhaps I'd get lucky.*

Long story short...I get real hot, and after an hour and a half, possibly two hours I hit the +300 dollar mark! This run was highlighted by a hand in which I split a pair of nines and ended up with five bets out (resplit/double down) all of which I won.

Now here's the thing: In all my fantasy/planning/practice on the computer during this year, $300 has always been my magic number. I've always told myself that if I hit $300 I'd either (A) quit right there and be on the next bus out of town, or (B) cash it in for green, hope for a miracle and try to double it at a $25 table. Guess what I did, here in the Resorts International Casino with 300 dollars in chips sitting in front of me (I had long since pocketed my original $120 buy in)? You guessed it. None of the above.

Choice C: "Just one more bet." I lost and yes, *friends, I do believe that I lost the next 12 hands in a row. And* yes, *I ripped through the $300 faster than I could ever have imagined, and* yes *out came my $120 buy in and* yes *there it went as well.*

Now, at some point I decided that if I lost the $120 after loosing my $300 I would quit and just get on the bus with the 100 dollar bill in my wallet (and my pride) intact. Of course, on my "last bet" I was dealt an 11! Double down time. Out came the hundred, and there went my pride. With the $100 now in chips in front of me, I decided that I'd just "play it out."

The thing is I knew that I was going to loose! *I had my moment, and it was $420 ago. This was just masochistic. And it was no longer fun. I wanted the dealer to deal faster. Shuffle breaks were* killing *me and when players hesitated in their decisions I wanted to scream, "Play the damn game!"*

I had tears in my eyes. I felt out of control. I felt like "that crazy guy at the table who went nuts" that everyone talks about.

In the back of my mind, I thanked God that I had the sense to leave my credit cards and ATM card home, and that I bought a round trip ticket. Yes, the inevitable happened: I walked out of Resorts with seven bucks in my pocket. Now I felt very lonely and I wished I were home. I got to the Showboat bus terminal at ten minutes to nine and I waited for my 9:30 bus. The 40 minutes was an eternity, and the bus ride was not fun either. I couldn't sleep and the word "loser" repeated endlessly through my mind. I tried to take some solace in the fact that I know that people much smarter, or

greedier, or shrewder than myself have done much worse.... I lost a measly
200 bucks. Big deal. People have lost it all—homes, wives.

Still, I had lost control, and it was frightening. It did not feel good.
Blackjack was no longer a fun break from reality. I wish that I'd have just
lost right away, than I could at least say: "Bad cards, nothing I could do."
This loss was all my *fault. I told my fiancee and my parents today, all of*
whom told me to not be too hard on myself, it's happened before, and it will
happen again. That's why and how casinos exist. They all said that I could
decide to either quit playing blackjack or take this as a challenge to focus
solely on the mental/discipline aspect of the game. Frankly I'm not sure
what I'm going to do. This game may be tougher than I am. I know full well
that my method of play is based on luck. I also know and understand the lim-
itation of my bankroll and of basic strategy. The intent of this [article] is just
to share my experience.

9

This, That, and Other Things

I think I can cover the overarching advice of this book in one carefully constructed, though rather long sentence. Here goes:

To sink Spanish 21, you must employ the full Armada Strategies, which include the Armada Play basic strategy to reduce the house edge to .82 percent; the Armada Ruse to gain the *monetary* edge with comps; and proper Armada money-management systems, including when to head for the door, in order not to get caught up in the casino mania that so many players fall prey to. Whew!

Yet, I realize that some other issues might also be of interest to my readers—issues that continually come up in my discussions of blackjack and other table games. The first issue that usually pops up in any discussion of casino games is the issue of selecting a table at which to play. The following question was used in my book, *Bold Card Play: Best Strategies for Caribbean Stud, Let It Ride and Three Card Poker!* but it is just as applicable to Spanish 21. With a few small changes, I have therefore adapted it for our purposes.

Would the technique called TARGET work for finding tables that are friendly to the players? I understand this is a technique used by blackjack players to find tables that favor them. What about "charting" tables as some craps authors recommend? Would this work in Spanish 21?

The TARGET technique that you are talking about is indeed a highly controversial method of trying to find "player-biased" tables in blackjack. It is the blackjack equivalent of charting tables in craps. TARGET was created by gaming author, Jerry Patterson, for the blackjack shoe games, which are, according to Patterson, not shuffled properly (properly = randomly) and thus lend themselves to prolonged bias either in the dealer's or the player's favor. Most blackjack authorities dismiss the TARGET concept (some quite violently—Patterson has been called all manner of names by his fellow blackjack writers) because it is unprovable mathematically or by computer simulation. You either buy into the premise or you don't. TARGET is a leap of faith.

Some of the ingredients in TARGET—for example, looking for tables where players have plenty of chips in front of them (this shows that they've probably been winning), or where cigarette ashtrays are full (this means people have been playing a long time, which probably means they've been winning), or where people seem happy (happy people are probably winning)—can indeed be used in Spanish 21 to pick a table. There is a reservation to doing this—*when in doubt, follow the math.* For example, even if two happy people are playing at a table and there are four empty seats at that table, while the table next to them has only one chair open with several less-than-happy players, go to the table that has more people, even if they aren't all that happy. You do not want to put yourself into a position of playing an enormous number of hands at a negative-expectation game, even one as good as Spanish 21. That's following the math. In Spanish 21, the first priority is to get to a full table where the game is significantly slowed down and then to slow your participation even further by taking bathroom breaks, referring to the traditional strategy chart for basic strategy, hemming and hawing and so forth.

TARGET and other "charting table" techniques fall into a category of playing techniques that I consider thusly: *All other things being equal, if it doesn't hurt you to follow the method, then follow it.* It is in fact much nicer coming into a game where players have been winning—it certainly feels good. So, you have two tables side by side and one has six people who are cursing, foaming, frothing, and demented-by-their-incredible-losing streaks and the other table has six people who are counting their chips, smiling, singing songs of praise to the gods of their choice—then you'd be an idiot not to go to the empty chair at the happy, smiling, singing table. You would always play the proper Armada Strategies for all the games and you would always play based on your bankroll and the size of the bets you can afford to make. However, with that in mind, it certainly can't hurt you to look around for crowded tables with happy people. (Note: I would personally avoid the tables with the ashtrays loaded with butts because it means either the waitresses aren't clearing the tables properly or that you'll be breathing through a nicotine fog during your playing session.) There is also another factor for Spanish 21 as well—you might not have much of a choice of tables in some casinos because the game is still relatively new. There may not be all that many tables to begin with!

Would a Martingale or a Grand Martingale work against Spanish 21?

No. The Martingale type wager, which is a double-up-after-you-lose system, is best used (I use the word "best" in terms of the worst of two evils!) in 50-50 situations or those that are close to it. Since you probably lose about 48 percent of your bets at Spanish 21 and only win about 43 percent, doubling after a loss is not a good idea. Actually, it is never a good idea but some players enjoy the excitement of the Martingale because it gives them a lot of little wins and usually (only!) a few devastating losses over time. In the end, the math of gambling says that you will lose the exact same percentage of money that you would have based on the house edge—no matter what betting scheme you use. What makes the Martingale undesirable from my point of view is the fact that you have to be extremely strong to weather those few devastating losses, which wipe out whatever little wins you've accumulated. If that's your speed, then sail away with a Martingale. If, on the other hand, you are like me—you don't mind a lot of little wins, you just mind *any* devastating losses—then for you the Martingale is not a good way to go.

A Grand Martingale, which is a double-your-bet-*and*-add-one-unit-after-you-lose style of betting is even more dangerous than its cousin as you'll hit the house edge that much faster. I thoroughly cover the Martingale styles of betting in both *Guerrilla Gambling: How to Beat the Casinos at Their Own Games!* and in *Spin Roulette Gold: Secrets of the Wheel!* Suffice it to say that while limited Martingales might be fun—say one, two or a maximum of three steps—attempting a full scale assault on the casinos using this system is fraught with peril and pain. At a normal Spanish 21 game, where the house minimum to maximums are $10 to $1,000, you will hit the house limit in just seven consecutive losing hands as you can see from this chart.

1-Step: $10	Total loss: $10
2-Step: $20	Total loss: $30
3-Step: $40	Total loss: $70
4-Step: $80	Total loss: $150
5-Step: $160	Total loss: $310
6-Step: $320	Total loss: $630
7-Step: $640	Total loss: $1270

Since the house limit is $1,000, you can't go any higher than the $640 bet. In addition, there may be times when you'll want to double down. Picture being in the hole for $630, then putting up a bet of $640 and receiving an 11 against a dealer's 6. Despite the fact that in the long run this is a winning hand for the player, in the short run you could find yourself destroyed if you lose that double down. When you get to the upper reaches of any Martingale, you just have too much riding on too few decisions to make it a good wagering system.

Would a positive progression betting system, as advocated by Walter Thomason in his The Ultimate Blackjack Book *(Carol Press), work at Spanish 21?*

Walter Thomason is one of my favorite gaming writers—despite the fact that I can't bring myself to endorse his idea of positive progression betting over card counting in shoe games. (Positive progressions are the exact opposite of Martingales—you increase your bet according to a set pattern only when you've won a hand or several hands in a row.) I have read Walter's excellent book and he has spoken to me on a number of occasions about his style of play. Walter tells me he has been quite successful with his positive progressions. I don't doubt that he has been because I know Walter to be an honest guy. He talks about his wins and losses openly and I've never found him exaggerating either. I once took up his challenge to play a few days using his style of positive progressive betting. I went to Atlantic City because the shoe games of Atlantic City are supposed to be perfect for progressions. As the theory goes, shoe games run hot and cold (at least they seem to in *retrospect*) but I just couldn't bring myself to do the progressions that Walter's system called for *when* they called for them. Basically I chickened out.

Here's why.

When the count of any given shoe was becoming increasingly more positive *and I was winning*, putting up more money as a part of the progression was not much of a problem. I would be putting up more money anyway whenever I had the edge (whether I was winning or losing) so doing it according to a progression system didn't cause me any major tremors. However, when I was betting into a *low count* I "fowled" up the progression and put up my smallest bet—even if I had won three or four hands in a row! I was chicken. I just couldn't overcome a lifetime of card counting and playing according to the count. My hand just couldn't put up more money in a negative count.

Even when I was winning in shoes that had gone into the basement, I just couldn't increase my bets. I am not opposed to putting a red chip on top of a couple of greens as the count descends in the hope that I'm hitting a streak (meaning a clump of big cards). That's a kind of progression, I guess, but it is the chicken kind. When the counts are low, the casino has bigger edges over you. That is a mathematical certainty. At any given moment in a low count, you have a good chance of having *just experienced* a small winning streak because the high cards came out. Still, betting the streak as opposed to the count just goes against my grain. As we have seen with Spanish 21, high cards favor the player *as they come out*. Once they are gone from the shoe the player is behind the eight ball. I trust the computer simulations and the math of blackjack over anything else—although I am not a religious fanatic about it. I do think there are ways to overcome even negative expectation games such as craps and roulette by *physical* means as opposed to betting systems. So I'm not a purist by any means. But I have had too much success playing blackjack the traditional card-counting way to abandon it—I'm a creature of habit and one habit I have come to really enjoy is having a slight edge over the house!

So, do I recommend positive progressions at Spanish 21? Yes and no. If you are winning and you have a comfortable lead, then a small progression might be just the thing to give you one of those epic wins. If the small progression goes awry early on, you can always reduce your bet back down to its original amount and flat bet the game, or take a break. The mathematical analysis of positive progressive betting shows the same results as the mathematical analysis of negative progressive betting—the casino will take the *exact same amount of money* as the house edge indicates over the long run regardless of the betting scheme employed.

One more thing—if you do employ a positive progression, make sure the casino pit person scoring your play notices those times when you increase your bets. This will help your comp rating and give you a return on your progressive investment.

Why would anyone play any negative expectation game, even one that is as close as Spanish 21, when they can play games such as regular blackjack, poker or video poker where it's possible to get an edge?

In my young and arrogant days, I used to ask myself that very same question. If you can get an edge at a given game, the way you can at blackjack, why not do it? Now having spent the better part of the 1980s and the 1990s analyzing and studying casino games and those who play them, I have come to a simple conclusion—and for one thousand dollars I'll tell you what it is—just kidding. Here it is: people play casino games for various reasons, such as the thrill of competition; to win money, to have a chance to win big money; to enjoy the supercharged atmosphere of the casinos; to get an adrenaline rush, or a dopamine rush (see the next chapter). The games they play suit their temperaments of the moment. Some people enjoy the elegance of baccarat; some love the heart-thumping action of craps;

some the leisure of roulette, still others the intense decision-making of real, live, casino poker. Still others enjoy the knowledge that they can get small edges (and be considered, therefore, experts!) at such games as video poker and blackjack. Scratch a casino player and you find many of the above reasons for playing—including one I've left out—fun. People play the games they like because these games are fun. You might not think that it's fun playing into a staggering house edge of 5.26 percent at a non-biased American roulette wheel (nor do I), but some people just love the game. For many people, playing is just as important as winning. To some other people, winning is the main thing. Most people are a mixture of all of the above: they have fun, they get rushes of various chemicals into their systems (yes, there is such a thing as a gambler's high), they want to win, maybe win big, and they like the atmosphere of the casinos. I am in the "I want to win money" first category but I now recognize that not everyone shares my essential mania for beating the casinos. Still, just about anyone with a modicum of intelligence when given a choice of playing a good strategy at their favorite game or playing a bad strategy at that very game, will (I hope) prefer to play the good strategy. If the sale of books on casino play is any indication, all people are not necessarily interested in putting in the time and effort to get small edges over the casino, but hundreds of thousands are indeed interested in learning the best possible strategies for their games of choice. So while winning might not be the only thing they are interested in, it certainly ranks among the top reasons to play.

10

The Psychology and Chemistry of Gambling

When I was a long-distance runner, before my knees gave out and my belly grew to rounded proportions, I used to delight in tweaking the noses of my more restrained acquaintances by solemnly telling them that I was a drug addict. There would be an inevitable pause, a long silence, as the individual took in this remarkable statement made by one who looked so damned healthy—and then I would quip: "Yep, I'm addicted to my own endorphins." We'd have a hearty laugh and my acquaintance would go away shaking his head at my little joke. Endorphins, indeed.

In fact, I *was* addicted to those endorphins, powerful chemicals that the brain releases during strenuous exercise that can soothe sore muscles and take a troubled mind into the nirvana of the fabled runner's high. The truth was that when I didn't run I didn't feel like myself. I was often moody and irritable. But when I ran, after five or six miles or so, ah, the world was all butterflies and flowers, nectar and honey, and I was just this feel-good machine pumping and pulsating through the woods. And when I raced in those mini-marathons of ten or more miles, I was chemically back in ancient Marathon, a Spartan gladiator taking on all comers, dizzied by the dismay of my foes and dazzled by my own strength and endurance. I was so alive and my light brightened the world!

Those runner's years are long past. I now power-walk (it's really called "power-waddling") and look to the casinos for that runner's high. In fact, I am now convinced that gambling in a casino is every bit as pleasurable, every bit as life enhancing, exhilarating and *endorphic* as running long distances or racing in mini-marathons.

Competitively, you are no longer challenging some skinny accountants who hit the trails in the early morning before hitting their ledgers for the rest of the day. You are no longer facing off against women and men who might never have competed in anything more intense than hunting for the right date for their prom in high school. In short, when you pit your puny self against the mighty casinos, you are no longer squaring off against a mirror-image of you as is done in most human competitions. No, when you gamble in the casinos, you are taking on no less than the Olympian gods of fate. The casinos are literally Nemesis and the sheer dread and joy we mortals feel when running against those gods—win, lose, or draw—cannot be understated but must be underscored.

Casino gambling is fun the way that sex with the love-of-your-life is fun; the way that good food on an empty stomach is fun; and the way that fine wine to a discerning palate is fun. But it is also fun the way laying waste to the village of your enemies was fun; the way challenging mammoths and saber-toothed tigers was fun; and the way waiting for the exact moment to harpoon that whale was fun. Megabucks meet Ahab!

Please do not discount the fact that psychologically, in some atavistic archives of our brains, most casino gamblers are intuitively cognizant of the fact that our current crop of casino games have rich historical antecedents. In the past our ancestors looked to dice to help them ferret out the will of the Almighty and when they "rolled them bones" the well-being of their own bones might have very well been at issue. All cards have their origin in the Tarot and while today's dealers merely divine a simple message (you won that hand or you lost that hand), the dealers of the past divined the very will of the Divine: "Sorry, but the cards foresee that tomorrow Magog seizes the city and decimates your people! The good news is that you won't see it because there's a spear with your name on it in the beginning of the battle!"

Yet, we are living in a scientific age and any ramblings about gods and goddesses, fate, free will and divination, must now inevitably wend their way through a Midas-sized maze of scientific research. The scientist says: "Don't tell me that when those prophets fasted for forty days and forty nights, that God then gave them visions. They were hallucinating because their brains had been deprived of food and were deteriorating." The mystic has been reduced to the neurochemical and the psychology of winning athletes has been reduced to which one has the better twitch-muscles.

So too with casino gambling.

Challenging the gods? Phooey! Here are the facts as our new religion, science, sees them.

According to Professor Marvin Zuckerman of the University of Delaware, a leading authority on the causes and effects of risk-taking in humans, some people are "sensation seekers" who crave "varied, novel, complex and intense sensations and experiences." Gamblers and other risk takers fall into this category. According to his studies, men tend to be slightly more sensation seeking than women, but both men and women tend to peak in their sensation seeking in their late teens and early twenties. In fact, some of this sensation seeking might actually be genetic in nature as studies with identical twins reared apart suggest. Evidently, some of us were born to rattle toys and others of us to rattle dice.

However, while Zuckerman looks to personality traits to characterize sensation-seeking, other scientists are looking at the very chemistry of the brain to discover the source of why one man's exciting craps game is another man's occasion to nap and still a third man's occasion to self-destruct.

According to the latest research, our neurotransmitters—a fancy term for the host of chemicals that transmit sensations and thoughts within our brains—are responsible for the excitement and pleasure we experience when we place our money at risk. In fact, they are responsible for the pleasure we feel no matter what we do—be it listening to a symphony by Beethovan to jumping into a mosh pit at a Megadeth concert. Indeed, one neurotransmitter in particular—dopamine—seems to be the Janus-faced master of our pleasures and orchestrator of our pains. When a craps player looks to the heavens and calls upon the gods in that heart-thumping moment between picking up the dice and rolling the dice, what is really taking place is an explosion of dopamine in the *nucleus accumbens* (the primitive pleasure center) of his or her brain. When those dice are released and the point number is hit, the craps player is bathed in the glow of a chemical high every bit as real and every bit as powerful as the runner's high I used to experience so long ago.

It is not an indictment of casino gambling to say that it is wonderfully addictive in the same sense that running is wonderfully addictive. To paraphrase the great Greek philosopher Epicurus, people should desire to maximize pleasure and to minimize pain.

That's *normal.*

Certainly, casino players know that the casino experience is pleasure personified and that trips to the wonderful world of Dame Fortune send the dopamine flowing through their *nucleus accumbens* aplenty.

That's *fun.*

However, for a small percentage of casino players the rush of dopamine heralds the onrush of personal doom. For these cursed few, casino gaming doesn't bring that "challenge the gods" heady thrill of victory or the "I'll get you next time, Zeus" agony of defeat; instead, like Cassandra, to these cursed few, casino gaming brings hopelessly self-destructive self-indulgence.

As there is a qualitative difference between sipping a fine wine in a fine restaurant and guzzling gallons of muscatel from a bottle in a brown-paper bag behind a fast-food joint's dumpster, so too is there a difference between the pleasures of waltzing with Lady Luck and the agony of being slam-danced by her. Unfortunately, for the cursed few that genes or Fate have selected, the surge of dopamine is so intense, so pleasurable, so necessary for a sense of well-being that come hell or Noah's flood, they will gamble every penny they have to satisfy the dictates of their appetite for dopamine. Before we shake our heads in disgust, let us realize that this is not so different from those long-distance runners who cannot control their desire to run, run, and run some more. Through shin splints, cartilage damage, blood in their urine, bone spurs and kidney breakdown, some runners become modern-day Jobs, suffering endless torment for a brief brush with the divine—in this case, their runner's high.

Although the self-righteous prophets among us might want to burn the casinos in fire and brimstone—forever preventing those of us who *are not* sacrificing our children to Molech to pay for our pleasures—these same prophets might as well ban running.

It is in the nature of man—chemically, psychologically, and, yes, spiritually—to dare, to push the limits, to gamble on this, that, or the other thing and to ultimately feel damn good about it, too. It's built into our hearts, it's built into our souls, and, if science is correct, it's built into the very structures of our brains.

You can bet on it.

Glossary

Ace: Valued as 1 or 11.

Ace Adjustment: The variation in bet size based on the number or proportion of aces remaining to be played. A technique that can enhance regular blackjack advantage play but is not as potent in Spanish 21.

Ace-Five Count: A simple card-counting system where the player keeps track of the aces and fives only.

Ace-Jack Bonus: Some casinos offer various bonuses for Ace-Jack of selected suits.

Ace Poor: A lower than average number of aces remain in the unplayed cards.

Ace-Rich: The remaining cards have more aces, proportionally, than normal.

Ace Side Count: Keeping track of the number of aces played separately from you counting system. Not really worth the effort at Spanish 21.

Act: The persona adopted by some card counters to give the impression that they are not skilled or expert players. In Spanish 21, the Armada Ruse is your "act" when using the traditional basic strategy card to make you look like a foolish player.

Action: The total amount a player bets over time at a given casino game. Used as a standard of judgment for casino comps.

Action Player: A player who bets big and/or plays the highest house-edge bets. Sometimes used as a euphemism for "dumb" player.

Advantage: The percentage edge that the player has over the casino or the casino has over the player.

Advantage Player: In the past, it used to mean a cheat but now means anyone who can get an edge over the casino even by legal means.

Anchor: The player who sits to the right of the dealer and is the last to act on his hand. Sometimes referred to as the "third baseman."

Armada Play: The basic strategy to be used against Spanish 21 that tells the player what to do with each hand versus every dealer upcard.

Armada Ruse: Looking like a normal player with a 2 to 3 percent disadvantage while playing the Armada Play basic strategy that reduces the house edge to .82 percent. Also, reducing the casino's edge by cutting the total number of hands played.

Automatic Shuffling Machines: Machines that shuffle the cards for the dealer. These machines are used to speed up the games and allow the casino to cut more cards out of play in order to thwart counters.

Backliner: A person who places a wager on another player's betting square.

Back Counting: To count cards while not playing. This is a technique used by guerrilla gamblers to only bet when they have the edge.

Balanced Count: A card-counting system where all the numbers ultimately add up to zero. The Hi-Lo that is recommended in this book is a balanced count.

Bank: The person who covers a bet in a game. In most casino games, the bank is the casino itself. Also, one of the three bets at baccarat.

Bankroll: The total amount of money a player has that is used for gambling. Also called a gambling *stake.*

Bar: The banning of an individual from playing in a casino. Used by the casinos against cheats and expert players alike.

Barber Pole: A bet consisting of different colored chips all mixed together. Trick often used by card counters to cover the amount of money they are betting.

Base Dealer: A dealer (card mechanic) who deals from the bottom of the deck. Not a problem when playing against a shoe as you do in Spanish 21.

Basic Strategy: In blackjack, the best possible play of any player hand against any dealer upcard. Basic strategies have been formulated by computer to be used for all possible player hands versus all possible dealer upcards in all possible black-jack games. The Armada Play is a basic strategy for Spanish 21. In other games, basic strategy means the best play available.

Bet: Name for any wager at any game.

Bet Blind: To bet without seeing your cards.

Bet Ratio: The ratio of the highest bet to the lowest bet that a player is making.

Bet Sizing: To vary the amount of one's bet based on one's advantage at that moment. In regular blackjack this is a useful technique. In Spanish 21 it is rare to have any edge—even with card counting.

Bet Spread: The lowest bet that a player is making compared to the highest bet that a player is making.

Bet Strategy: The scheme a player uses to vary his bets.

Bet Variations: To change the level of betting. This can be done by bet sizing or by betting progressions or betting regressions.

Bias: The tendency of a game to favor either the dealer or the player over an extended period of time. While a few experts think that table bias in blackjack is a real phenomena, most blackjack authorities dismiss the idea.

Black Action: A bet made with a black ($100) chip.

Blacks: Chips valued at $100.

Body Time: For purposes of comping, how much time your body has been at the table. Some of this time, you will not have money at risk.

Bonus: A special payment for select hands at Spanish 21.

Break: To go over 21. Also known as busting.

Break down a bet: Separate chips by the various denominations. Used by dealers to accurately pay off bets.

Bull: Another name for the ace in poker.

Burn Card or Burn Cards: To bury a card at the beginning or during a blackjack round. Used as a device to prevent card counters from getting an edge.

Bury a Card: Place a card in the middle of the deck.

Buy in: Exchanging cash for chips at a table. The original amount of cash exchanged for chips in the beginning of a player's action.

Cage: The cashier's area of the casino where chips are exchanged for cash.

Camouflage: To play in such a way as to cover up your real abilities. In regular blackjack, it is to cover the fact that you are a card counter. At Spanish 21, it is to cover the fact that you are playing the Armada Strategies.

Capping a Bet: Adding more chips to a bet that has already won. This is also known as *past posting.*

Card: Also referred to as a *player rating card* or *comp card,* the plastic card that looks like a credit card that casinos use to keep track of a player's action.

Card Clumping: The tendency of groups of cards to stay together for prolonged periods in shoe games because of insufficient shuffling by the dealer.

Card counting: Keeping track of the cards that have been played or are in the other players' hands in order to gain an edge over the casino and/or to determine the best strategy for the playing of one's hand. Effective in blackjack but only a theoretical possibility at Spanish 21.

Card Dauber: A person who marks the cards for purposes of cheating.

Card Mechanic: A skilled manipulator who can control the cards as he or she shuffles. Technique used strictly for cheating.

Casing: An old term for keeping track of the cards that have been played from a deck or shoe.

Casino Advantage: The edge, usually shown as a percentage, that the house has over the player.

Casino Host: The person responsible for seeing that high rollers are treated with the dignity and graciousness their wallets merit.

Casino manager: The person responsible for seeing that the various games of the casino are handled properly.

Casino Win Rate: How much of all the money bet that a casino wins at a given game. In traditional blackjack, the win rate hovers around 15 percent—sometimes a little more, sometimes a little less.

Centerfield: The middle betting position at the center of a table that has seven players.

Chasing losses: Increasing your bets in order to recoup what you've lost. A very dangerous way to play.

Check rack: The tray that holds the chips for the game.

Checks: Another name for chips.

Choppy game: A game where neither the house nor the player has been winning consistently. Opposite of a streak.

Clocking: Keeping track of the results of a given game to determine how or whether to bet.

Cold table: Any table where you have been losing.

Color up: To exchange smaller denomination chips for larger denomination chips at the table.

Comp: Stands for complimentary. Casinos give certain inducements such as free and discounted rooms, food, and shows for certain levels and durations of play. Comps play an important role in the Armada Strategies as generous comps can turn the game in the player's favor.

Concealed Computers: Devices used by some blackjack players to get an advantage over the house. These are now considered in almost all gambling jurisdictions as cheating devices and some states have imposed heavy jail sentences for their use.

Conversion Factor: How the running count is divided or multiplied in order to arrive at the true count. This is based on the number of cards that have been played.

Cooler: A deck or shoe of prearranged cards inserted into games by cheats.

Counter Catcher: The individual hired by a casino to catch card counters at blackjack. Thus far, no "Armada Sinkers" have been hired to thwart the Armada Strategists.

Counter Measures: The steps the casinos take to protect their games against card counters.

Counting Down a Deck: Keeping track of the count as the cards are dealt. Some individuals practice counting down a deck at home, believing that speed is important. It isn't. No dealer can deal as fast to players as one player can deal to himself.

Cover: How a card counter disguises the fact that he is counting cards. Sometimes this cover is changing the style of one's decisions or betting so as not to be too pre-dictable, or changing one's appearance so as not to appear too intelligent. Looking stupid is the best possible cover for any advantage player.

Credit line: The amount of credit that a casino will extend to a player.

Credit manager: The person responsible for who gets credit and for how much.

Crew: The personnel who work a game.

Crimp: A bend in a card put there by a player or dealer for identification purposes. A cheating technique.

Crossroader: A casino cheat.

Cut Card: The plastic card that indicates the shuffle in a shoe game.

Cut the deck: To divide the deck before dealing. Often done by a player.

DAS: Abbreviation for double after splits.

Daub: To cheat at cards by placing a small amount of paint or ink on the card for the purposes of later identifying it.

Dead hand: A hand that can no longer be made. A hand that has been discarded.

Dead table: A table where no one is playing.

Deal: To give out the cards.

Dealer: The casino employee who staffs the games offered. The person who distributes the cards.

Dealer Bias: A deck or shoe that has been favoring the dealer.

Dealing Seconds: Dealing the second card in the deck until you need the first card to either make a good hand or to break a player's hand.

Deck: A regular deck is composed of fifty-two cards from the two through the ace. There are four separate suits: spades, diamonds, hearts and clubs. In Spanish 21, the 10-spot cards have been removed so that deck is a forty-eight card one.

Desperado: A gambler who plays foolishly. In Spanish 21, the Armada Strategist wants the casino raters to think of him or her as this type of gambler.

Deuces: The two-valued cards.

Discard Rack: The plastic, upright receptacle for cards that have already been played in shoe games.

Double-Deck Game: A game played with two decks usually dealt by hand.

Double Down: To double the size of your bet and receive only one card. At Spanish 21 you can double on any number of cards and you can double for less than the initial bet if you wish.

Double Down Rescue: Player may surrender his or her original bet but keep the double-down bet in action. This rule does not apply after the hand is busted.

Double Exposure: Blackjack game where both of the dealer's cards are dealt face up. Also known as Face Up blackjack.

Double Up System: This is also known as the Martingale family of wagers. Player attempts to get all his previous losses back by increasing the size of his previous bets (usually by doubling). Results in a lot of little wins and a few devastating losses that wipe those wins out.

Drop Box: The box hanging from the table where the players' cash is deposited after exchanging it for chips.

Dummy Up: To shut up. Some casino pit people will say to chatty dealers: "Dummy up and deal."

Dumping: A table that is losing money to the players. Usually means that the dealer has been busting.

Early Surrender: Rarely-found option in blackjack that allows players to forfeit half their bet, even if the dealer had a blackjack.

Edge: Having an advantage in a game.

Eighty-six: The same as barring a person from playing in a casino.

Eldest Hand: The player to the dealer's immediate left.

Element of Ruin: The likelihood that a player (or team) will lose his entire bankroll. Usually expressed as a percentage figure. If you have, for example, a 1 percent element of ruin, you will theoretically lose your bankroll 1 percent of the time on average. In negative expectation games, with a bankroll that is never added to from time to time, the element of ruin could be considered 100 percent since the longer you play the more assuredly you'll lose.

End Play: The play of the hands at the end of a deck or shoe when one's advantage is known.

Even money: A wager, the winning of which pays off at one to one. That is, if you bet one dollar, you win won dollar. In the casino an "even-money" bet does not mean that the odds are actually 50-50.

Expectation: The amount, usually expressed in a percent or in dollars, that a player should win or lose over an extended period of time. This is based on the game and the player's skill level.

Exposed Card: A card that is inadvertently shown during the play of the hand.

Eye-in-the-Sky: The camera, usually in bubbles, located throughout the casino that videotapes the action. Used for the protection of both the players and the casino.

Face cards: The king, queen and jack. Also known as *picture cards.*

Face Down: Games where the first two cards are not exposed to the other players. Players may touch the cards to see them. Most hand-held single and double-deck games are dealt this way.

Face Up: Games where the cards are dealt with their values visible. Players may not touch the cards and must indicate their decisions by hand gestures. Most shoe games are dealt this way.

False Cut: A cut of the cards that leaves them in the same order that they were in as before.

Fair Game: A game where neither the casino nor the player has the edge.

Favorable Deck: A deck whose remaining cards favor the player. Also known as *positive deck.*

First Base: The seat at the table immediately to the dealer's left.

First Basing: Attempting to see the dealer's hole card when he checks for a blackjack.

Five Count: Keeping track of the number of fives that have been played.

Flashing: To show a card to a player. Dealers can flash their hole cards and, in hand-held games, players can flash their cards to the other players.

Flat Bet: A bet that is paid off at even money or a bet that is the same amount hand after hand.

Floorman (floorperson): The individual responsible for supervising several tables in a pit.

Fluctuation in Probability: Numbers or hands appearing out of all proportion to their probability. A short sequence that favors the house or the player. A mathematical term that is translated as good or bad luck depending on whether the fluctuation favors the player or the house.

Front Loader: A blackjack dealer who unknowingly shows his hole card as he places it under the upcard.

Front Money: Money previously deposited with the cage and used by the player to draw markers against.

Fun Book: Coupon book used by the casinos to encourage play. Also contains discounts for drinks, food, novelties, etc.

Gambling stake: Amount of money reserved for gambling. Same as *bankroll.*

George: A good tipper.

Glim: A concealed mirror used for cheating at cards.

Grand Martingale: A wagering system where you double your bet and add one extra unit after a loss.

Greens: Chips valued at $25.

Grifter: A scam artist.

Grind: A derogatory term for a small roller. A player who bets small amounts. The term used to describe what the casino edge does to a player's bankroll.

Grind Down: The casino winning all of the player's money due to the advantage it has on bets.

Grind Joint: A casino that caters to low rollers.

Grind System: Any system that attempts to win small amounts frequently against the casinos.

Guerrilla Gambling: The combination of smart play and hit-and-run tactics to beat the casinos at their own games.

H-17: Abbreviation for a game where the dealers hit their soft 17s.

Hand: A player's cards in a card game.

Hand-Held Game: A game where the dealer deals from his hand and not from a shoe. Most single and double-deck games are hand-held games.

Hand Mucking: A casino dealer who palms and then substitutes cards into a game at the appropriate time.

Hard Hand: A blackjack hand that doesn't have an ace or one with an ace where the ace must be used as 1 or 11 but not both.

Head-to-head: To play against the dealer with no other players in the game. Sometimes referred to as *heads up* or *face-to-face* or *one-on-one*.

Heat: Surveillance by the casino of a suspected card counter. Or pressure put on a card counter (or any good player) during the course of a game in order to get him or her to leave the table. This usually happens before the casino "asks" a player to leave the premises.

High-Low or Hi-Lo: A level one counting system that gives the value of plus one to the 2, 3, 4, 5, and 6, and gives the value of minus one to the ace and 10-valued cards.

High Low Pickup: A cheating method in blackjack where the dealer picks up the cards in a high-low alternating manner.

High roller: A player who plays for large stakes.

Hit: To ask for another card in blackjack.

Hit and Run: Using guerrilla gambling techniques against the casinos.

Hold: The actual amount the casinos take from their games.

Holdout Shoe: A shoe that has been tampered with to allow the dealer to deal seconds.

Hole Card: The second card dealt to the dealer in blackjack that is face down. Any face down card.

Hot Player: A player who has been winning.

Hot and Cold System: A wager on the side that won previously. Another name for the streak method of betting.

Hot Table: A table where the players have been winning.

House Edge: The advantage, usually expressed as a percentage, that the casino has over the player at a given game. This advantage is usually attained by not paying back the correct odds on a wager or by structuring games so that the casino wins more decisions than the players. Sometimes the edge is a combination of both.

House Odds: The payoff that reflects the casino's tax on your winning bet.

House person: A dealer who is unusually concerned with the casino's profits. A dealer who enjoys watching the players lose. A dealer who identifies with the casino. Sometimes derogatorily referred to as the *house pet* or *house plant.*

Hustler: A gambling cheat.

Index or Index Number: The count necessary to deviate from basic strategy at traditional blackjack.

Insurance: A side wager at blackjack, for up to half the original wager, that the dealer has a blackjack when he has an ace showing.

Irregularity: A departure from the standard procedures at a given game. What players might suffer from when they've lost more than they can afford to.

Jackpot: A grand payout for hitting a certain premium hand.

Joint Bankroll: Two or more players combining their bankrolls so as to wager against a larger bank. Good method for traditional card counters. Might be marginally effective in garnering more comps at Spanish 21.

Joker: A wild card that can usually be substituted for any card in the deck in designated games. Usually resembles a court jester.

Juice: The percent the casino takes out of a winning bet. Also the name for any commission charged on a bet either before or after winning it. A person with pull in the casino is said to have juice.

Junk: Bad hands.

Junket: A trip organized and subsidized by a casino to bring gamblers to play at the games.

Junket Master: The person in charge of a junket.

Kelly Criterion: A betting system utilizing the knowledge of a player's advantage at any given point in the game. The player bets the proportion of his bankroll that represents his advantage.

Key-Card Concept: An advanced strategy in blackjack that is based on the idea that at certain times in a game one or two denominations are even more important than the count. For example, no matter how high the count, if there are no more aces on the deck, there will be no blackjacks. Spanish 21's removal of the 10-spots is based on the key-card value of 10s in the game.

Kibitzer: An individual who is not playing at a given game but is giving unwanted advice.

Laydown: Another name for a bet. Also, someone who quits in the middle of a game.

Layout: The design imprinted with the various bets of a given game.

Level: An honest game.

Level-One System: A card counting system that uses +1 or -1 as the value of the cards that are counted.

Locationing: The ability to memorize a group of cards so when one of the group appears the player will know which cards are to follow.

Long End of the Bet: The side that must pay off more than it collects.

Long run: The concept that a player could play so often that probability would tend to even out. That is, you would start to see the total appearance of decisions or events approximating what probability theory predicts. A "long-run" player is one who plays a lot!

Lose All to a Natural: A rule found in Europe and some other areas that stipulates that should the dealer have a natural, all bets—including double downs and splits—are lost. A horrible rule. Run if it ever appears in the New World.

Mark: An individual who has been or is going to be cheated. A sucker.

Marked Cards: Cards that have been physically altered in subtle ways so that either a cheating dealer and/or a cheating player can read them when they are face down.

Marker: The check the player fills out before receiving credit at a casino table. A promissory note or IOU.

Martingale System of Wagering: Doubling one's bet after a loss in an attempt to make back all your losses and a small win. Dangerous.

Match Play: A casino promotion where the players are given special chips that they can bet. They are paid off in regular casino chips if they win.

Maximum Bet: The highest bet allowed at a table.

Mechanic: Anyone who can manipulate the cards.

Mimic the Dealer: A playing strategy where the player imitates the dealer who plays by the house rules. Not a good style to play for either traditional blackjack or Spanish 21.

Minimum Bet: The smallest bet allowed at a given table.

Mirroring: Using any shiny object to get a peek at the dealer's hole card.

Money at Risk: Money that has been wagered and can be lost.

Money Management: The methods a player uses to conserve his bankroll from ruin.

Money plays: The call that alerts the dealer and the pit that the player is betting cash and not chips.

Mucker: Anyone who uses slight-of-hand techniques to cheat at cards or other games.

Multiparameter Count: A card-counting technique where you keep a separate count of the cards that count as zero in your normal card-counting system.

Multiple-Deck Game: Blackjack played with more than one deck. These games give the house more of an advantage over the players. Also, any shoe game with more than one deck.

Multiple Hands: Playing more than one hand at blackjack during a given round of play.

Nail: To catch someone cheating. "We nailed him."

Natural: A blackjack, an ace and 10-valued card on the first two cards.

Negative Count: A count that favors the casino.

Negative progression: Any system of wagering where you increase bets after a loss.

Nickel: Five dollar chips—usually red.

No action: A call made by a dealer that the casino will not cover a particular bet or that a particular deal doesn't count.

Odds: The likelihood of a given event happening.

Off the Top: The first hand after the shuffle.

On the Square: A game that is honest.

Open: To make the first bet.

Opposition Betting: Betting against the count. Used by card trackers and clump players.

Overbetting: Betting more than your bankroll or your psychology can handle.

Paddle: The tool used to push the money into the drop box.

Paint: A picture card.

Painter: A name for an individual who cheats at cards by daubing them with a small amount of paint. Also known as a *Picasso*.

Pair: Two cards of one denomination. For example: two aces.

Palm: To conceal money or chips in one's hands.

Parlay: To double one's bet after a win.

Past Posting: Placing a wager after a decision has been reached. Usually done by *capping* a bet.

Pat hand: Any hand in a card game that does not require getting additional cards. Seventeen through 21 on the first two cards are all pat hands.

Peeking: A dealer checking to see what his hole card is when he has a 10-valued card and/or an ace up.

P.C.: The house edge expressed as a percentage.

Penetration: How deeply the dealer deals into a deck or shoe at blackjack. For traditional card counters, this is a key variable in judging the beatability of a given game. If you are not counting, it is better to have bad penetration because the more cards cut out of play, the more the dealer deals, the fewer hands the player plays, the less the player loses, and the more comp credit the player gets without the attendant risk.

Penny Ante: A game played for small stakes. It used to be literally a penny to ante, which means to get into the round of play.

Pinching: Illegally removing chips from one's bet after an unfavorable decision.

Pit: An area in the casino consisting of a number of table games.

Pit Boss: The individual in charge of a pit.

Player's Card: Plastic credit-card type card that is used by the casino to identify and track a player's play.

Ploppy: The very worst kind of player. Plays his or her own strategy and is not adverse to sharing his or her "secrets"—for free!

Plus-Minus System: Another name for the Hi-Lo system or High-Low system of card counting. Cards are given a +1 or a -1 value.

Positive Count: Any count that favors the player.

Power of the Pen: The ability on the part of some casino executives to issue hotel comps to players.

Preferential Shuffling: Shuffling the cards when the remaining deck or decks favor the players and dealing the remaining cards when the deck or decks favor the house. Devastating method that some casinos might use to "cheat" the players without technically cheating.

Premium players: A casino term meaning big bettors or players with big credit lines.

Press: To increase one's wager after losing.

Producer: A casino term for a player who loses often and for large sums. This individual is a producer of profits for the casino.

Progressive Jackpot: A jackpot that continues to increase as players play until one player hits the necessary hand to win it.

Prop: Another name for a *shill.* A person employed by the casino to play a game to generate action. Most often used in baccarat and poker.

Proportional Betting: To bet a portion of your money based on your advantage or some other betting scheme.

Proposition Bet: Any bet that is a long shot and carries a heavy house edge. Usually side bets that require an additional sum of money are prop bets.

Push: Casinoese for a tie where neither the player nor the casino wins the bet.

Quarters: Chips valued at $25—usually green.

Random Shuffle: To intermix the cards in such a manner that no intentional clumping takes place. In any random shuffle there will be streaks of low cards and high cards but these will not be predictable. A single-deck that has just been put into play requires seven shuffles to be randomly shuffled.

Rank Count: A card-counting system that only keeps track of one or a couple of cards values.

Rating: Evaluating a player's play for the purposes of comps.

Rating Card: The card used for rating the player. Same as *player's card.*

Reds: Casino chips worth five dollars.

RFB: Stands for room, food and beverage. The highest level of comps that a player can get. Includes free rooms, free meals, shows, parties, limos, and sometimes even plane fare.

Riffle: Splitting the deck in two and shuffling both sections into each other.

Riot Act: Being told by the casino in no uncertain terms that your play is not wanted and that, if you return, you will be arrested. This is being "read the riot act."

Ruin: Losing your bankroll. The probability of losing every penny of your bankroll. Same as *element of ruin.*

Rule card: The card that explains the rules for a given game.

Running Count: The unadjusted or raw count that tells you the ratio of high cards to low cards.

Rush: A quick winning streak.

Scam: Any scheme to defraud a casino or player.

S-17: Abbreviation for dealer standing on all 17s.

Scanning: The quick perusal of the cards that have been played for the purposes of determining advantage.

Scam: Any scheme to defraud a casino or a player.

Scam Artist: An individual who specializes in defrauding casinos or players.

Scared money: Money that you are playing with that you can't afford to lose.

Scratch: In hand-held games, the player's brushing of the cards along the felt to indicate he or she wants a hit.

Seconds: A cheating method where the second card and not the top card is dealt. The top card is saved to either make a hand or break a hand.

Session: A predetermined or given period of time or money won/lost or number of decisions that a player uses to establish when to play and when to go.

Session Stake: The amount of money a player has set aside for a given period of play. Usually a percentage of the total bankroll.

Shift boss: The individual in charge of a casino during a given work shift.

Shill: An individual employed by the casino to play games that are being underplayed. Also known as a *Prop.*

Shoe: The box that holds the decks for a card game.

Short Deck (Short Shoe): The removal of certain cards from the deck or shoe to increase one's chances of winning. In Spanish 21, the casino has removed the 10-spots to increase its edge over the players.

Short End of a Bet: The side of the bet that has to pay off less than it will win.

Short Odds: Anything that is less than the true odds payoff of a bet.

Short Run: The limited amount of time during any given session when probability theory will seemingly be skewered by streaks and fluctuations.

Shuffle Check: Some casinos require the floorman to check the shuffle before the dealer puts the cards in the shoe. This check is to insure that the cards are thoroughly mixed so shuffle trackers are thwarted.

Shuffle Point: The number of cards or decks that a dealer deals out before he or she shuffles the deck or shoe. Usually indicated by a plastic card inserted into decks.

Shuffle Tracking: Watching as the cards are being shuffled to memorize and later locate certain groups of cards.

Shuffle Up: Technique used to thwart card counters. The dealer will shuffle after every deal or when a suspected card counter enters a game and/or raises his bets.

Side bet: A second bet, in addition to the normal bet(s), on a proposition at a table game.

Side Count: To keep a separate count of cards other than those in your basic counting system. Generally, counting systems that value the ace as zero will keep a separate count for them.

Single-Deck Blackjack: The best game in the casino if the rules are liberal and the dealer deals out enough cards.

Slug: A group of cards that have been prearranged in a given order and inserted in the deck. Any group of cards inserted whole into the deck. Also a rounded piece of metal that is inserted into a slot machine that mimics a coin.

Snapper: An archaic term for a blackjack. A *red snapper* is a blackjack composed of two red cards. Also a term for the dealer who audibly snaps the cards as he or she deals. To the trained ear, this snapping can sometimes indicate that the dealer is dealing second.

Soft Hand: A hand at blackjack where the ace can be valued as 1 or 11.

Soft players: A term for poor players.

Split: To make two different hands from a pair.

Spook: A player—usually at another table—who sees the dealer's hole card in blackjack and relays that information to the player who is playing against the dealer.

Spread: The difference between the minimum and the maximum bet that a player makes at a given game.

Squares: A game that is on the level or honest. "This game is on the square."

Stacked deck: A deck of cards that has been prearranged in a certain order for cheating purposes.

Stand: To keep the cards you have. Not to draw any more cards.

Steaming: A player who is visibly upset and is playing recklessly at a table.

Stiff: A bad hand in blackjack. Also, not to tip the waitress or waiter who serves you drinks.

Strip: Las Vegas Boulevard. Three miles of casinos.

Strip Shuffle: Dealer pulls a group of cards off the top, inverting the order of the groups.

Surrender: A blackjack option where the player may give up half of his or her bet. Player loses full bet if the dealer has a blackjack, however. Sometimes known as *late surrender.*

Sweat: Casino personnel who get upset when a player is winning are said to "sweat" their games. Also, a player who is losing and is worried.

Table Hopping: Moving from table to table in a casino.

Take Down: To remove a bet before a decision is made.

Tapped Out: To lose one's entire bankroll.

TARGET: Controversial method of selecting a table at which to play in blackjack.

Team Play: Anywhere from two to several to dozens of players working together to beat the casinos.

Tell: Any unconscious signal that allows you to know what another player or the dealer has in his or her hand.

Third base: The position to the dealer's right. Player who acts last on his hand.

Three Sevens: Bonus hand in Spanish 21.

Three straight: Three cards—6, 7, 8—to a straight. Bonus hand at Spanish 21.

Toke: Another term for a tip for a dealer.

Toke hustler: A dealer who tries to get the players to tip him.

Tom: Casinoese for a poor tipper.

Topping the deck: Palming cards for the purpose of cheating.

Tough Out: The Captain's term to describe a skilled player who doesn't defeat himself. (see *Beat the Craps Out of the Casinos: How to Play Craps and Win!*)

Tournaments: Blackjack games where the players compete not just against the dealer but against each other for cash and prizes.

True Count: The adjusted count that reflects the count-per-remaining decks.

True odds: The actual probability of an event happening.

Twenty-One: Another name for blackjack.

Unbalanced Count: A card-counting system where all the values do not add up to zero.

Underground Joint: An illegal casino.

Unfavorable deck: A deck or shoe that favored the casino over the player.

Up card: Any card that is dealt face up.

Vic: Sucker. Short for victim.

Vig or vigorish: The casino tax on a bet. The amount taken out of a player's winning wager or the amount of the commission paid on a wager. Also known as *juice.*

Virgin principle: The superstition that a beginner will have good luck. Also known as *beginner's luck.*

Wager: Another term for bet.

Warp: A bent card.

Wash: One bet cancels out another bet. Also, the process of mixing fresh cards together on the top of the table without lifting them.

Wild Card: A card that can be used for any other card in the game.

Win Rate: How much a player or casino can expect to win based on the house edge or lack thereof.

Zero: A loser.

Recommended Gaming
Authors

I love reading other gaming writers and I do recommend to anyone who is interested in truly becoming a strong player, no matter what game you like to play, that you build a gaming library or read certain writers in the various gaming publications. Here are my favorite gaming authors in alphabetical order. Some I read for pleasure and background anecdotes; some I read to learn strategies from. Some of these writers are controversial and are attacked by others of these writers. But in my opinion they are all worth reading, although not all the advice of every writer is necessarily to be followed. For example, I love reading the late Sam Grafstein's books on craps but I never play his way. Still, he's fun to read. But if you want to create a gambling library, these writers would be important to have on your shelves...right next to *all of my* books of course! Many of the following writers have only one or two books to their names; some have many books, some write little booklets, some write reports. Some have no books (as yet) but are currently making their names in magazines (including my own *The New Chance and Circumstance*). Some write about one or two games; some write about comps; some deal in the math of gambling, and some write about everything. I recommend that you read them all. In the past there were very few worthwhile books or even readable writers in the gaming field. Today it's a whole new ballgame. Next to each name will appear a code to indicate what the individual writes about.

(ALL) means they write about everything; (B) = baccarat; (BJ) = blackjack; (C) = craps; (CL) = color; (COM) = comps; (L) = legal issues; (M) = math of gambling; (OTG) = other table games; (P) = poker; (R) = roulette; (S) = slots; (T) = tournaments; (VP) = video poker.

A. Alvarez (P)
Ian Andersen (BJ)
Russell Barnhart (M, R)
Frank Barstow (ALL)
Thomas Bass (R)
Steve Bourie (CL)
Julian Braun (BJ)
Doyle Brunson (P)
Richard Canfield (BJ)
Bryce Carlson (BJ)
Mike Caro (P)
Carlson R. Chambliss (BJ)
Jeff Compton (COM)
Dwight Crevelt (S, VP)
Anthony Curtis (ALL)
Michael Dalton (BJ)
Bob Dancer (VP)
Bradley Davis (VP)
Larry Edell (C)
Lenny Frome (VP, OTG)
Ken Fuchs (BJ)
John Gollehon (ALL)
Peter Griffin (BJ, M)
Sam Grafstein (C)
John Grochowski (ALL)
Jim Hildebrand (S)
Anthony Holden (P)
Lance Humble (BJ)
Marvin Karlins (CL)
Stanley Ko (OTG)
Alan Krigman (ALL)

Mason Malmuth (BJ,M,P)
Eddie Olsen (BJ)
Darwin Ortiz (ALL)
Alene Paone (ALL)
Jerry Patterson (ALL)
Dan Paymar (VP)
Mario Puzo (CL)
Fred Renzey (BJ, P)
Lawrence Revere (BJ)
John Robison (S, VP)
Stanley Roberts (BJ)
Thomas C. Roginski (BJ)
I. Nelson Rose (L)
Max Rubin (COM)
Don Schlesinger (BJ)
Frank Scoblete (ALL — but of course!)
Jean Scott (COM)
Edwin Silberstang (ALL)
David Sklansky (M, P)
Arnold Snyder (BJ)
Maryanne K. Snyder (ALL)
John Soares (CL)
Lyle Stuart (B,C)
Henry Tamburin (ALL)
Alan Tinker (AKA: A.Tinker Bell) (T)
Walter Thomason (ALL)
Edward O. Thorpe (BJ, M)
Ken Uston (BJ)
Olaf Vancura (ALL)
Barney Vinson (CL)
Allan N. Wilson (ALL)
Stanford Wong (BJ, T)
Alan Wyckes (ALL)
Herbert O. Yardley (P)